WILFRED THESIGER IN AFRICA

WILFRED THESIGER
IN
AFRICA

EDITED BY CHRISTOPHER MORTON
AND PHILIP N. GROVER

Published to accompany
Wilfred Thesiger in Africa: A Centenary Exhibition,
Pitt Rivers Museum

Harper
Press

PittRivers
MUSEUM

Harper*Press*
An imprint of HarperCollins*Publishers*
77–85 Fulham Palace Road
Hammersmith, London W6 8JB
www.harpercollins.co.uk

Visit our authors' blog: www.fifthestate.co.uk
Love this book? www.bookarmy.com

First published in Great Britain by Harper*Press* in 2010

1

A catalogue record for this book
is available from the British Library

ISBN 978-0-00-732524-5

Design by Terence Caven

Printed and bound in Spain

The editors wish to express their deep gratitude to William Delafield and the William Delafield Charitable Trust for their invaluable support towards the production of this book.

The editors also wish to thank in particular: Benedict Allen, Adrian Arbib, Sir David Attenborough, Terence Caven, Jeremy Coote, Elizabeth Edwards, Ian Fairservice, Camilla Hornby, Bruce Hunter, Richard Johnson, Schuyler Jones, Rob Judges, Sarah Lewis, Alexander Maitland, Laura Marshall, Michael Meredith, Alistair Morrison, Gwen Mortimore, Michael O'Hanlon, Malcolm Osman, Jamie Owen, Robyn Parker, Jonathan Pegg, Colin Pennycuick, Imma Plana, Suzy Prior, Robert Prys-Jones, Heather Richardson, Torsten Seidel, Michael Upchurch and Cathy Wright.

Contents

Chapter 1

Wilfred Thesiger in Africa

ALEXANDER MAITLAND

The greatest traveller of the twentieth century and one of its greatest explorers, Sir Wilfred Thesiger is most famous for his journeys in Arabia and his sojourns among the Marsh Arabs in Iraq. Yet fifty of Thesiger's seventy years living, travelling and exploring in remote places were spent in East and North Africa. Thesiger was born in 1910 at Addis Ababa and lived there until 1919 when his family returned to England. Throughout his life, Thesiger continued to revisit Ethiopia, which he preferred to call by its former name Abyssinia. In 1944 he achieved his boyhood ambition of living and working in Ethiopia; however, this was in wartime when he felt that he might have been employed more usefully elsewhere. From 1960 to 1963 and from 1968 to 1977 he travelled each year, on foot, using camels to carry baggage, in northern Kenya. From 1978 to 1994, he settled at Maralal in Kenya's Eastern Rift Valley Province, among the cattle-owning Samburu. It was there, among his Samburu and Turkana adoptive 'families', that he wished to spend his final years.

From 1919 to 1933 Thesiger was educated in England, first at St Aubyn's preparatory school in East Sussex, and later at Eton College, followed by Magdalen College, Oxford, where he read Modern History. Thesiger's 1930 autumn term at Oxford was interrupted by Haile Selassie's coronation, to which he was invited both by the Emperor himself and the Foreign Office as Honorary Attaché to HRH the Duke of Gloucester, who headed the British Mission.

Dressed in a morning suit that contrasted dully with the dress uniforms and medals worn by others in the Duke of Gloucester's party, Thesiger felt conspicuous and ill at ease. Soon, however, he was absorbed

by the splendours of the occasion and wrote: 'You could easily imagine
yourself back in the days of Sheba.'[1] For ten days he took part in ceremonies, processions and banquets. Finally he watched the Patriarch
crown Haile Selassie (Fig. 1). The Emperor under the state umbrella
then emerged into the cathedral square, where he received homage
from chiefs in brilliant robes and lion's mane headdresses, their shields
ablaze with gold and silver. Even at that moment Thesiger was conscious
that such long-revered customs, rites and traditions were doomed to
disappear. 'Already there were a few cars in the streets. There had been
none when I was a boy' (Fig. 2).[2] Seeing the priests dance in the cathedral, he wrote to his younger brother, was 'a sight never to be forgotten
. . . you can't even try to describe such scenes as I have seen in a letter'.[3]

  After the ceremonies were over, Thesiger set off alone to hunt big
game, following the Awash River as far as the hot springs at Bilen.
Looking back, he felt convinced that this month in a country inhabited
by the Afar (Danakil)[4] tribes had been the 'most decisive' month in his
entire life.[5] He described this journey in the first chapter of *Arabian
Sands* (1959):

My first night in camp, as I sat eating sardines out of a tin and watching my Somalis driving the camels up from the river to couch them by the tent, I knew that I would not have been anywhere else for all the money in the world. For a month I travelled in an arid hostile land. I was alone; there was no one whom I could consult; if I met with trouble from the tribes I could get no help; if I were sick there was no one to doctor me. Men trusted me and obeyed my orders; I was responsible for their safety. I was often tired and thirsty, sometimes frightened and lonely, but I tasted freedom and a way of life from which there could be no recall.

The opportunity of hunting and travelling in Abyssinia had given Thesiger a tremendous thrill. His family ties with the country dated from 1868 when his grandfather, the Hon. Frederic Augustus Thesiger, had served as Deputy Adjutant-General under Sir Robert Napier during the campaign to release a British consul and other captives imprisoned at Meqdala (Magdala) in Abyssinia by the increasingly harsh and erratic Emperor Tewodros (Theodore) II. As General Lord Chelmsford, Frederic Thesiger later commanded the British force in South Africa, in 1879, during the Xhosa and Zulu Wars. Although he finally defeated the Zulu army at the battle of Ulundi, Chelmsford

FIG.2 Procession through the streets of Addis Ababa during the coronation ceremonies of Emperor Haile Selassie. Thesiger described the scene as 'an odd mixture of East and West'. *Addis Ababa, Ethiopia. Photographer unknown. November 1930.*

would be remembered not for this crucial victory, but for the massacre of more than 1,300 of his troops by the Zulu army at Isandhlwana. At Wilfred Thesiger's home in the Welsh borders were the assegais, clubs and shields that his grandfather had brought back from Zululand. Memories of conflicting emotions stirred by the Zulu relics caused Thesiger to write in *The Life of My Choice* (1987): 'my grandfather . . . had shattered the Zulu army at Ulundi . . . but I never begrudged those peerless warriors their earlier, annihilating victory over a British force on the slopes of Isandhlwana'.[6]

Abyssinian impressions

FIG.3 Wilfred Thesiger's father, who from 1909 held the post of Consul-General at Addis Ababa, arriving at the palace residence of Emperor Menelik. *Addis Ababa, Ethiopia. Photographer unknown. December 1909.*

Thesiger's father, Wilfred Gilbert Thesiger, died in 1920. The third son of Lord Chelmsford, he joined the consular service in 1895, and was posted first of all to Lake Van in eastern Turkey, followed by Taranto, in southern Italy, Belgrade, and then St Petersburg. In 1907 he was posted to Boma in the eastern Congo. In Belgrade he proved his ability and courage by running single-handed the British Legation, after anarchists had murdered King Alexander and Queen Draga. In the Congo, Wilfred Gilbert investigated Sir Roger Casement's shocking reports of atrocities inflicted by Belgian officials on native workers employed in the plantations. He performed these duties so efficiently that, in 1909,

FIG.4 Interior of one of the round huts, or *tukuls*, which served as the British Legation prior to the construction of a new building in 1911. *Addis Ababa, Ethiopia. Photograph by Wilfred Gilbert Thesiger. Circa 1910.*

he was appointed HM Consul-General and Minister Plenipotentiary in charge of the British Legation at Addis Ababa, which his immediate predecessor, Captain John Harrington, had helped to establish only a few years before the Thesigers' arrival there (Fig. 3).

On 21 August 1909, Captain the Honourable Wilfred Gilbert Thesiger DSO married Kathleen Mary Vigors at St Peter's Church, Belgrave Square, London. The couple arrived at Addis Ababa in early December, after they had trekked for a month with mules, across the Tchercher Mountains, from the railhead at Dire Dawa in eastern Abyssinia. Wilfred Patrick, eldest of the Thesigers' four sons, was born at 8 p.m. on Friday 3 June 1910 in one of the circular, thatched mud huts known as *tukuls*, which originally housed the British Legation. These huts were less primitive than Thesiger's descriptions suggest. The better furnishings were shipped from England, and then transported by camel-caravan across the Danakil Desert. The wattle-and-daub walls of the Thesigers' *tukul* were tastefully papered and decorated with framed pictures, and the exposed roof lathes were interlaced with coloured ribbons (Fig. 4). Kathleen Thesiger thought them 'enchanting' and described the Legation *tukuls* as 'wonderfully spacious and most comfortable to live in'.[7] The single-storey building housing the new Legation

FIG. 5 Wilfred Thesiger with his mother and younger brother Brian in front of the new Legation building. *Addis Ababa, Ethiopia. Photograph by Wilfred Gilbert Thesiger. Circa 1913.*

had a pedimented façade and shuttered windows. Sited in a compound that according to Kathleen was the size of St James's Park in London, it was completed in 1911, and became the family's home for the next eight years (Fig. 5). Thesiger's parents were both energetic gardeners and the gardens they laid out and planted have remained to this day very much as they left them.

Thesiger's early upbringing in Addis Ababa was immensely significant, and, he maintained, affected the whole course of his life from then on. His brother Brian, a year younger, who joined in everything Wilfred did, remained almost untouched by their shared experiences. The two youngest children, Dermot and Roderic, were aged 5 and 3 when the Thesigers left Abyssinia early in 1919. As a result, neither the country nor its people left any lasting impression on them.

Thesiger remembered vividly sitting on the Legation steps in the evening, and listening to his father read aloud from his favourite books. Among them were *Jock of the Bushveld* (1907), Sir Percy Fitzpatrick's story of a dog's adventures in the South African wilds; *A Sporting Trip through Abyssinia* (1902) by Major P. H. G. Powell-Cotton; and *African Nature Notes and Reminiscences* (1908) by Frederick Courteney Selous. Edmund Caldwell's beautiful drawings in *Jock of the Bushveld* may have inspired

Wilfred Gilbert Thesiger's sketches of big game in his letters to Wilfred and Brian. These books fired Wilfred's boyhood passion for big game hunting, and encouraged a lifelong fascination with African peoples.

During visits to Addis Ababa, Arnold Wienholt Hodson, who served as a consul in Abyssinia from 1914 to 1927, enthralled Wilfred with tales of big game hunting and tribal warfare. Besides Hodson's books, *Seven Years in Southern Abyssinia* (1927) and *Where Lion Reign* (1929), Thesiger possessed photographs taken by Hodson on safari, many of them captioned in Hodson's handwriting. According to a letter written by Thesiger's father, and his own recollections, the urge to hunt originated in Thesiger's earliest childhood. He had tried as a toddler to knock down birds in the garden with a bat and an empty cartridge-case his father had given him, perhaps to play with instead of a ball. Aged 3, he had watched his father shoot an oryx, and remembered how the wounded antelope galloped madly away before it collapsed in a cloud of dust. He remembered later sitting up with his father, near the Legation, anxiously waiting for him to shoot a leopard that never appeared. He said: 'My father enjoyed hunting big game, but he wasn't very successful. He did some shooting while he was in the Congo and [hunted] in Abyssinia as well as India and Kenya. I liked being there with him and it was probably doing this that got me started.'[8]

Among his other memories of childhood in Abyssinia were vague impressions of camels and tribesmen at waterholes; of white-robed priests with their prayer-sticks and silver drums dancing before the Ark of the Covenant at Timkat, or Epiphany; watching in horror, one day when he and Brian were riding, as their escort dismounted from his horse, and, in doing so, stabbed himself accidentally through the shoulder with his lance; seeing Ras Tafari's victorious army march their prisoners past the Empress Zauditu, after the battle at Sagale north of Addis Ababa, which crushed the Revolution in 1916 (Fig. 6 overleaf). He also remembered a boy-soldier, in Ras Tafari's army, being carried shoulder-high, and how he would have given anything to change places with him. The deep impression made on him by such extraordinary experiences he felt certain was a key to understanding the adventurous life he would lead, years later, in Africa and elsewhere.

Stimulated by his upbringing in Abyssinia, Thesiger's powers of observation were no doubt focussed and sharpened by his passion for

big game hunting and bird life. As his fascination with birds grew, he progressed from merely shooting, to studying birds and recording their behaviour. Lying awake at night in his preparatory school near Brighton, he often pictured his home in Addis Ababa, and the brilliant green-and-chestnut bee-eaters and crimson touracos fluttering among the trees in its large garden. Throughout his life, Thesiger was always more sensitive to visual images than he was to sounds. He was tone-deaf; and he confessed that music, however beautiful or melodious, meant little more to him than a 'jumble of noises'.[9] For the same reason, bird-song and the call-notes of birds may have been essentially meaningless to Thesiger – although he insisted these never failed to evoke for him atmospheric, vivid memories of the African bush. Having no ear for music, he was not particularly receptive to nuances and variations in people's voices. As a result, his publishers complained that his attempts to reproduce direct speech were seldom convincing. Thesiger's com-panions in Morocco said that he spoke French haltingly, and with a bad accent. Yet his spoken Arabic was fluent and slightly flavoured by the accent and intonation of Darfur's Muslim tribes and the dialects of the Bedu with whom he travelled in Arabia. He enjoyed listening to drums and to the rhythmic stamping of tribal dancers' bare feet; but, unlike his brothers, he never learned to dance. In his autobiography *The Life of*

My Choice (1987), he recalled with dry self-mockery his clumsy effort at dancing with the wife of Sir Angus Gillan, the Sudan's Civil Secretary, in the 400, a fashionable Mayfair nightclub.[10]

The Afar (Danakil) and the Awash River

In *The Danakil Diary* (1996) Thesiger describes in more detail the hunting trip he made to Bilen after the coronation of Haile Selassie:

> I had gone down there to hunt, but this journey meant far more to me than just the excitement of hunting . . . [T]here had been the constant and exciting possibility of danger . . . with no possibility of getting help if we needed it. I had been among tribesmen who had never had any contact with a world other than their own.[11]

Among the Oromo (Itu Galla), Thesiger had 'an unpleasant feeling . . . of being in a hostile country . . . constantly being watched from the hilltops'.[12] That 'wonderful' month gave his boyhood dreams a thrilling reality and made him even more determined to live a life of 'colour and savagery'.[13]

After the coronation in 1930 Thesiger had intended to hunt in the Sudan, but was advised against this because of the expense and difficulty of arranging the necessary permits.[14] Instead, Colonel Dan Sandford, who had served for five years with Wilfred Gilbert Thesiger and farmed near Addis Ababa, suggested that Wilfred should spend a month hunting in the Danakil country. While in Addis Ababa, Thesiger also met Robert Ernest Cheesman (1878–1962) who had been a consul at Dangila in Abyssinia from 1926 to 1929 and had published an account of his earlier adventures, *In Unknown Arabia* (1926). Cheesman recollected Thesiger saying to him, 'I want to do some exploring. Is there anywhere I could go?' When Thesiger showed no interest in 'cold countries' of the Polar regions, Cheesman suggested the Awash River which vanished somewhere in the Danakil Desert. Writing in 1959, Thesiger seemed to imply that having decided to explore the Awash River, he approached Sandford for help with the hunting trip to Bilen;

not only to shoot big game but also to 'have a look' at the Danakil and get some impression of their country.[15]

During the month Thesiger hunted on the Awash, his headman on that occasion, Ali Yaya, made continual enquiries about the river on his behalf. According to the local Afar, the river ended against a great mountain in Aussa, a country of lakes and forests, forbidden to outsiders and ruled by a xenophobic sultan. Thesiger wrote: 'I had felt then the lure of the unknown, the urge to go where no white man had been, and I was determined, as soon as I had taken my degree, to return to Abyssinia to follow the Awash to its end and to explore the Aussa Sultanate.'[16]

The objectives of the expedition varied, owing to differing agendas set by its sponsors. According to the Imperial Institute of Entomology, its primary object was 'to collect material for the British Museum (Natural History)' and obtain data for the Institute 'respecting migratory locusts'. The Royal Geographical Society endorsed this, adding that Thesiger also wished 'to undertake surveys and photography'.[17]

Replying to a letter from Thesiger in April 1933, C. W. Hobley, a colonial administrator and authority on East Africa, gave advice and useful information for any geologist, ornithologist or anthropologist attached to the expedition, and suggestions for borrowing cameras and handling supplies of film.

> Cameras can be hired from various sources but I fancy only ciné-cameras & not ordinary ones – you might try the RGS for the latter. The Zool[ogical] Soc[iety] has a very nice hand ciné-camera, it cost £100, they might lend it to someone who was competent to work it, upon certain terms, if fully insured by the borrower against loss & damage, but I cannot say for certain . . . Films need special packing for hot countries . . . [18]

He added a caution: 'Your only hope of grants is to guarantee the scientific aims of the expedition, geographical research or mere exploration is not enough.' Hobley's advice on geology and ornithology, no doubt, partly explained why these aims took precedence over Thesiger's personal motives: 'to follow the Awash river into the fabulous Sultanate of Aussa and discover how and where it ended'.[19] Of vital importance to Thesiger were the challenges offered by the 'murderous' Afar, as well as the many hardships involved with the journey.[20]

Thesiger's story of his 1933–4 Awash expedition was first published by *The Times*, in a series of four articles, titled 'An Abyssinian Quest', dated 31 July and 1, 2 and 3 August 1934. The text of his lecture to the Royal Geographical Society in November 1934, 'The Awash River and the Aussa Sultanate', appeared in the *Geographical Journal* in 1935. Other versions appeared in *Arabian Sands* (1959), *Desert, Marsh and Mountain* (1979) and *The Life of My Choice* (1987). *The Danakil Diary* (1996), edited from the original notebooks he kept as a daily journal, gives the most detailed account of this journey, one that Thesiger regarded as the most dangerous he ever undertook. The reasons he gave for describing the expedition as excessively dangerous were: his youth and inexperience; the ever-present risk of being attacked by parties of hostile Afar warriors; the possibility of being murdered in Aussa; dying from heat and thirst during the last stage of his trek. Indeed, by the end of the journey fifteen of Thesiger's nineteen camels had to be abandoned, or had died of hunger and exhaustion. Thesiger never forgot the dogged dependability of some of those camels – Elmi, Farur, Neali and the 'great-hearted' Negadras – to whom he owed so much (Fig. 7).

In January 1935 the young French commandant of Dikil fort, Captain Bernard, was killed and mutilated by Asaimara Afar, less than nine months after Thesiger had stayed with him on his way to the coast. Thesiger was only too well aware how this tragedy could have happened

FIG.7 Wilfred Thesiger's party setting out from the Awash Station at the start of his 1933–4 expedition. *Awash Station, Ethiopia. December 1933.*

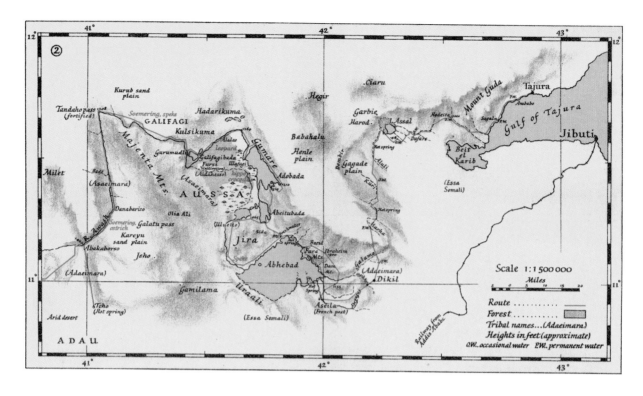

FIG.8 Map of the Awash River and the Aussa Sultanate, from Thesiger's account of his expedition published in the *Geographical Journal*.

to him and his followers. Instead, his expedition was successful. Having been granted permission by the Sultan of Aussa to cross his previously forbidden territory, Thesiger became the first European to map the Awash as far as Lake Abhebad, proving it was here that the river ended (Figs. 8 and 9). With the assistance of Omar Ibrahim, his middle-aged Somali headman, and local interpreters, Thesiger collected a lot of information about the Afar and their customs. While some of his photographs were poorly framed, due to his Kodak camera's damaged viewfinder, many were clear and informative.

Besides his notes and sketches describing the geography of the Awash River and features such as Afar burial sites, Thesiger collected seventy-six plant specimens and shot and preserved fourteen species of mammal including the *k'ebero*, the Abyssinian red wolf. His collection of 872 birds included 192 species and three new subspecies – an Aussa rock chat (blackstart) (*Cercomela melanura aussae*), a Danakil rock sparrow (*Gymnoris pyrgita dankali*) and a Danakil house bunting (*Fringillaria striolata dankali*). According to modern taxonomic methods, the latter two birds are nowadays generally not considered distinctive enough to merit recognition, and consequently have been sunk ('synonymized') into other, previously described subspecies; in this case the yellow-spotted

petronia (*Gymnoris pyrgita pyrgita*) and the house bunting (*Emberiza striolata striolata*).[21]

As well as skinning and preserving the animals and birds he shot, and interviewing the Afar, Thesiger carried out many other time-consuming and sometimes intricate tasks himself. While the expedition gave no template for the style of his later journeys, he admitted he had felt relieved when David Haig-Thomas – a companion whom Thesiger's mother had insisted he must take with him – dropped out, because of illness, after a preliminary journey in the Arussi Mountains (Fig. 10). Yet in his lecture to the Royal Geographical Society, and an article in *The Ibis*, Thesiger emphasized that he had been 'handicapped severely' by the absence of Haig-Thomas, who was the expedition's ornithologist.

FIG.9 Lake Abhebad where the Awash River ends. Thesiger later wrote: 'I had come far and risked much to see this desolate scene.' *Lake Abhebad, Ethiopia. April 1934.*

FIG.10 Wilfred Thesiger's camp at the Awash Station where David Haig-Thomas left him. *Awash Station, Ethiopia. November 1933.*

This he never repented. Some people who attended Thesiger's lecture, however, felt he should have shown more sympathy for Haig-Thomas and paid tribute to the research into Abyssinia's birds which Haig-Thomas had undertaken before he and Thesiger left England.

During the Awash expedition, Thesiger travelled in the same way his father had travelled in the past, 'as an Englishman in Africa'. He fed and slept apart from the men who accompanied him. He communicated with them sometimes directly but mainly through Omar, his headman. Thesiger admired and respected Omar, but in no sense did he regard him as a friend. He felt depressed in the railway station at Jibuti, saying goodbye to his followers, all of whom had proved loyal, 'utterly reliable', and had never questioned Thesiger's decisions 'however seemingly risky'. As for Omar, Thesiger wrote, 'I was more conscious than ever how much of my success was due to him.'[22] As a travelling companion, Omar had felt Thesiger was hard to equal.[23] Later – in the Sudan – Thesiger learned to treat his men as companions, rather than servants. By the end of the Awash expedition he already inclined towards this still highly unconventional practice – due mainly to the influence of Henry de Monfreid, a French pearl-fisherman and smuggler, whose books, *Les secrets de la mer Rouge* (1931) and *Aventures de mer* (1932), he had bought

at Addis Ababa and read at intervals throughout his journey. By the time he arrived at Tajura, Thesiger had fallen under de Monfreid's spell. Crossing from Tajura to Jibuti in a dhow, sharing the crew's evening meal of rice and fish, brought de Monfreid's romantic world alive (Fig. 11). At Jibuti Thesiger found de Monfreid's dhow *Altaïr II* 'anchored in the bay'.[24] He was told Henry de Monfreid was in France. Thesiger apparently did not know that de Monfreid had been deported by Haile Selassie after the publication in 1933 of his book, *Vers les terres hostiles de l'Éthiopie.* The *Altaïr*, whose Arabic name means 'bird', was for sale. On Hôtel d'Europe writing paper, Thesiger scribbled a brief summary of the vessel's running costs. For the *Altaïr* itself de Monfreid wanted £1,200. Fuel (crude oil), repairs, wages and food for the crew totalled £65 per month. The owner received 40 per cent of the income from pearl-fishing, the remaining 60 per cent was divided among the divers and the crew.[25] Thesiger wrote: 'I thought fleetingly of buying her and leading a life resembling [de Monfreid's], but reality took charge.'[26] The truth was that the son of a former British Minister at Addis Ababa, a friend of the Emperor, was never destined to live like de Monfreid, whom officials treated as an outcast, 'fishing for pearls off the Farsan isles and smuggling guns into Abyssinia through Tajura'.[27] Thesiger remained

FIG.11 Dhows at Tajura on the Jibuti coast, from where Thesiger sailed after his Awash expedition. This panorama of the bay is a composite image made from joining two different photographs of the scene. *Tajura, Jibuti. May 1934.*

loyal to his hero, despite the fact that Henry de Monfreid later served as a war-correspondent and alleged apologist for Mussolini during the Italian occupation of Abyssinia from 1935 to 1941. In 1942 de Monfreid was arrested on a charge of espionage and deported to Kenya. There he remained, a prisoner of war, until 1947 when he was repatriated to France.

The Sudan

In England as a boy Thesiger daydreamed continually of Ethiopia. By the time he went to Eton in 1923, he had made up his mind to join the Sudan Political Service. He accepted that it was somewhat unusual for a boy of 12 or 13 to have had such a definite plan for his future, and the determination to achieve it. There were, however, several good reasons for this. Thesiger said:

> The Sudan bordered Abyssinia. I felt that serving there would help me to get back to Abyssinia, where I wanted to be, whereas being somewhere like Nigeria wouldn't. Besides I had read books such as Abel Chapman's *Savage Sudan* (1921) and [John Guille] Millais's *Far Away up the Nile* (1924) and I was attracted to the Sudan by the prospects for hunting big game and getting among the tribes that lived on the Nile. It was the hunting and tribes and being close to Abyssinia [that] made me feel the Sudan was the right place for me.[28]

Never for a moment did Thesiger expect to serve somewhere like Khartoum or one of Sudan's cotton-growing areas. When he was fortunate enough to meet Charles Dupuis – the Governor of Darfur Province – at a friend's house in Radnorshire in 1934, he left Dupuis in no doubt as to the sort of adventurous life he hoped to lead. Thesiger had been interviewed by the Sudan Political Service that August and had been accepted, he felt certain, in large part due to the success of his recent Awash expedition. Dupuis, on the other hand, realized that despite his awkward manner and sense of 'ancient' virtues, Thesiger might well be an asset the Sudan Political Service could not afford to lose. When Dupuis discovered that Thesiger had been posted to the Wad Medani cotton-growing district, he urged Sir Angus Gillan, the Civil Secretary, to post him instead to Kutum in Northern Darfur. Dupuis assured Gillan that if he did not do this Thesiger would almost certainly resign.

Based at Kutum from 1935 to 1937, Thesiger served as an Assistant District Commissioner under Guy Moore, who encouraged him to ride camels and to treat the tribesmen who were with him not as his servants but as companions. Sitting on the ground beside his men, sharing their fire, eating from a communal dish, at first Thesiger felt self-conscious and even condescending. He soon, however, grew accustomed to this way of life and preferred it both on trek and at home. At Kutum, he replaced the trained Sudanese servants with a 14-year-old murderer from the town gaol.[29] Idris Daud of the Zaghawa tribe had been imprisoned after stabbing another boy in a scuffle.[30] Thesiger secured his release, paid the blood-money owed to the victim's family and put Idris in charge of his house. Idris became Thesiger's devoted companion. Guy Moore – with whom Thesiger got on extremely well – was often away, whereas Idris seldom left Thesiger's side (Fig. 12). On safari, Idris served as his gun-bearer and tracker, and when necessary as translator.

FIG. 12 Idris Daud, dressed in white, rolling up a tent with a Nuer porter. *Western Upper Nile, Sudan. 1938.*

He was an excellent shot, a dependable and fearless gun-bearer upon whom Thesiger could rely when he hunted dangerous game such as lion, elephant and buffalo.

In Northern Darfur, Thesiger shot thirty lion, most of which had been raiding cattle owned by the Bani Hussain and Kobé-Zaghawa tribes. Hunting by himself or joining in the tribesmen's pursuit of those lion, Thesiger saved many herders from serious injury or death. He wrote: 'you probably saved a couple of [them] from being killed or mauled and you were getting closer to them'.[31] He observed that, 'When hunting lion they expect to get at least one man mauled or killed. On one occasion a lion mauled twelve Zaghawa before they succeeded in killing him. When with them I have always spoilt the sport by shooting the lion.'[32]

In the Sudan's Western Nuer District, where he served from 1937 to 1939, Thesiger killed forty more lion, bringing the total number he had killed to seventy. In the Sudan Political Service's journal, *Sudan Notes and Records*, Thesiger described galloping down lion, bringing them to bay, dismounting and shooting them, if possible, before they charged. Galloping down lion had been a highly dangerous sport made popular by European settlers on the Athi plains of Kenya. Arthur Blayney Percival, Kenya's first Chief Game Warden, regarded it as 'the finest sport in the world'.[33] In *A Game Ranger's Notebook* (1924) Percival enthused: 'the race over country after [a lion] stirs the blood as no stalk can possibly do'.[34]

Thesiger was charged sixteen times, once at very close quarters by a lion which knocked him down. (Whether the lion actually did so, or whether a tribesman standing nearby, whom the lion had attacked, fell against him, Thesiger could never be sure.) This lion would probably have killed them both had Thesiger not managed to scramble to his feet and shoot it through the head with his .350 Rigby Mauser. Thesiger was convinced, if he went on hunting lion, his luck could not possibly hold. 'It became an obsession. I felt that if I kept on, one day a lion would certainly kill me. But the urge to keep hunting them was too strong to resist.'[35] At what stage Thesiger reached this conclusion, and indeed why he gave up after he had killed seventy lion, he does not tell us. It has been suggested that he lost his nerve: an explanation with which he vehemently disagreed. Perhaps he had wearied of hunting lion in the Nuer country, mainly as a sport. Hunting cattle-raiding lion in Northern Darfur had been more purposeful and far more dangerous, since these lion were often bold and very sly and offered Thesiger all the challenge and excitement he could possibly have desired.

In 1935, when 'Pongo' Barker, the Sudan's Game Warden, told him there were lion in Darfur, but that nobody had ever shot one, Thesiger vowed he would succeed where previously other men had failed. It seems clear from everything he said and wrote about his experiences in the Sudan that hunting lion meant more to him personally than hunting any other dangerous species of big game. Thesiger later read about certain totemic attitudes to lion described in *Pagan Tribes of the Nilotic Sudan* (1932), by anthropologists Charles and Brenda Seligman (from whom Hobley had urged Wilfred to seek advice on the Afar in April 1933).[36] Among the Niel Dinka tribe of the Upper Nile, lion were regarded either as ordinary animals or as man-eaters. Dinka clans of the lion-totem believed that man-eaters were not 'one' with themselves and should be killed on sight. On the other hand, the Dinka might feed ordinary lion with joints of meat, cut from a sheep, left at some distance from the village. The villagers prayed that the lion would come and feed off this meat, but if they did not the villagers would eat it themselves.[37] After one Dinka man had killed a lion, and sometime later another lion killed twenty of his cattle, the tribe refused to hunt the marauder whose depredations they considered a fitting punishment for the herdsman.[38] In the 1930s, throughout the Sudan, lion were classed as vermin and unlimited numbers could be shot without a licence. As an employee of the Sudan Political Service, Thesiger was entitled to a general licence to hunt specified varieties of game, at a reduced annual fee. Additional licences permitted sportsmen to shoot a maximum of two elephants each year. In the desert, south of Wadi Howar, he had stalked addax antelope (*Addax nasomaculatus*), whose meat he described as 'very fat and juicy'. He wrote: 'It is strange that this animal which never drinks and won't live anywhere but on the very edge of the true desert has the best flesh of any animal in the Sudan.'[39] In 1935, on the slopes of Jabal Ubor in the Jabal Maidob in Northern Darfur, he shot a Barbary sheep (*Ammotragus lervia*) with horns measuring twenty-eight and three-quarter inches over the curve (Fig. 13 overleaf); an inch longer than the official record for the Sudan. In the Western Nuer District between 1937 and 1939 Thesiger killed four elephant and twelve buffalo. Thesiger's game-book listed only twelve animals he judged 'worth recording'. Of course, he

FIG.13 Wilfred
Thesiger and hunting
party with the horns
of a Barbary sheep shot
in the Maidob Hills.
Northern Darfur, Sudan.
Photographer unknown.
1935.

had shot more than these (quite apart from the seventy lion he killed
over five years); but he was nevertheless adamant that he had taken care
to shoot 'selectively and seldom'.[40]

In *The Life of My Choice* (1987) Thesiger acknowledged the debt he
owed Guy Moore who, he wrote, had recognized from the start his
'craving for hardship and adventure' and his preference for remote
places.[41] 'I undoubtedly owe much of my later success as a traveller,' he
wrote, 'to his unobtrusive coaching. No other DC [District Commissioner]
would have sent me to the Libyan Desert to learn about desert travel
with camels under testing conditions.'[42] Moore's nostalgia for deserts,
and his admiration for tribes who lived there, deepened as he grew older.
Reading *Arabian Sands* in 1959, Moore wrote that it 'makes even my nos-
trils distend a little with past memories of barbaric glories'.[43] After he
retired to England, Moore often longed 'to return to the Desert and
poke the fire . . . with a dagger in that incomparable company that
gathers round it to share for a few hours the Peace of God'.[44] In 1964,
he inscribed for Thesiger a Christmas card showing the Three Wise Men
riding their camels across a moonlit desert: 'Silent their voyaging –

victory their quest/ Beyond the tumult in the city's breast/ Over the dune, sinew and heart to test/ Unshod to tread the Temple of God's Guest.'[45] Thesiger wrote that, in the Sudan, Moore – who had served in Iraq and spoke fluent Arabic – often referred to the desert as the 'High Altar of God'.[46] The letters he wrote to Thesiger after the Second World War were filled with yearning for a vanished past. Thesiger kept these letters, but admitted that he had found some of them disturbing and sad. Thesiger wrote in 1987: 'More important [than camels or desert travel], something decisive in my life, [Guy] taught me to feel affection for tribesmen. Ever since then it has been people that have mattered to me, rather than places.'[47] Thesiger was criticized for the phrase 'taught me to feel affection', on the grounds that affection cannot either be taught or learned. Did Thesiger instead mean that Moore had taught him it was all right to feel affection for tribal people? If so, this would make more sense. Thesiger confessed that he had found difficulty, to begin with, putting some of Moore's teaching into practice.

Sharing food and sleeping arrangements with his followers was something Guy Moore's contemporary Hugh Boustead (1895–1980) would never have done. Nevertheless, the well-being of Fur cultivators in his district had been Boustead's overwhelming concern. Years after he had left Zangili, the Fur tribe remembered him with admiration. Hugh Boustead believed that the welfare and happiness of tribal people depended on an improved standard of living that resulted from Western education and technology. Thesiger liked and admired Boustead, while observing (in exasperation more than disapproval) that, 'For all his versatility he was by nature conventional, holding firmly to English ways . . . he would never have worn native dress'.[48] Thesiger did not accept that Western education and innovations necessarily improved people's lives or made them happier than they had been in more 'primitive' conditions. He felt that, if anything, the reverse was true, and noted that Boustead never appeared to consider the possibility of damaging repercussions. Boustead's attraction to the African wilds never faded. On 12 June 1971 (aged 76) he wrote enthusiastically to Thesiger from Tangier: 'If I could get up to [the] Turkana [Lake] Rudolf country – I'd love it.'[49]

In August 1937 Thesiger trekked to Jabal Maidob (Darfur), accompanied by Mark Leather, a young officer from El Fasher who was later to be awarded the Military Cross, and in November of that year made the first of several journeys with his mother in Morocco. At Jabal Maidob Thesiger shot another fine Barbary sheep, a ram with thirty-one-inch horns, which surpassed his unofficial record shot in 1935. Thesiger praised Leather as 'an admirable companion . . . enthusiastic about everything, and desperately keen on his hunting'.[50] Leather enjoyed travelling with Thesiger too, and pictured him as 'a real "tough guy" [who] knows how to do things hard'.[51] Thesiger wrote to his mother:

> For those days I lived with the Maidob as I love living, moving where we would, sleeping under the stars, at one moment gorged on meat, the next with nothing but some flour and water, with no barriers between us. We had one unforgettable night when we came across some shepherds and spent the night with them. Everyone so free and natural. They played to us on their pipes round the fire far into the night, lads each of whom looked like Pan.[52]

Among Thesiger's most memorable experiences in the Sudan was a journey he made south-west from Jabal Maidob to the Anka wells. 'I sat or slept on a rug on the ground,' he wrote, 'with my few possessions in my saddle-bags, and enjoyed that easy, informal comradeship that this life and our surroundings engendered. It was my first experience of the infinite space of the real desert, its silence and its windswept cleanness.'[53]

Travelling with his mother that autumn in Morocco, he found a land that still retained something of its antique charm and mystery. There were no flights from Europe; Morocco could only be reached from there by rail and sea. From Marrakech, with its palm groves set against a backdrop of snow-capped mountains, the Thesigers visited Telouet, Taroudant, Meknes and Fez, whose setting among the hills he felt could only be compared with Istanbul seen from Pera, or Jerusalem seen from the Mount of Olives.[54] The Pasha of Marrakech, Thami al Glawi, gave Thesiger and his mother a banquet in his spectacular kasbah at Telouet in the Atlas Mountains (Fig. 14). In 1931, Kathleen Thesiger had married an elderly widower, Reginald Astley, yet she remained what she had always been to her son: a goddess without equal in his otherwise exclusively male pantheon. She was tireless, uncomplaining and interested in everything she saw. In her

guidebook Kathleen noted beautiful buildings, people and exotic scenery, using rather colourless phrases that masked her feelings of excitement and wonder.[55]

Among the Nuer on the Upper Nile – as in Ethiopia – Thesiger had lived and travelled 'like an Englishman in Africa'.[56] He enjoyed being with the Nuer, yet in their pagan society he felt unfulfilled, isolated and lonely. Travelling across the vast Sahara, he reverted easily to the freer, less encumbered life he had begun to miss increasingly since he had left Northern Darfur. At an encampment in Wadi Howar early in 1937 Thesiger first heard stories of Tibesti – a mountainous region of dormant volcanoes mostly in northern Chad – from Kathir, one of the Badayat tribesmen whom Guy Moore had recruited to watch for camel-raiders crossing the Sudan's northern frontier. The old man described huge mountains named Tu, 'many days' journey towards the setting sun'.[57] Thesiger felt sure that Tu must be Tibesti. He decided immediately he would go there. In April 1938 the Civil Secretary's office in Khartoum approved his journey; agreement from the French authorities followed in May. On 3 August Thesiger set off from Tini, Idris Daud's village, with a small party including Idris, and with Kathir, Thesiger's elderly Badayi informant as their guide. The first European to visit Tibesti, Gustav Nachtigal (1834–85), had arrived there in 1870

FIG.14 Kasbah at Telouet in the High Atlas Mountains, which Thesiger first visited with his mother in 1937. *Telouet, Morocco. 1937.*

from Fezzan (Libya). Tibesti had been explored and mapped by a French expedition led by Lieutenant-Colonel Tilho in 1925. No European, however, had approached Tibesti from the east across the Sahara, nor, to Thesiger's surprise, had any English traveller visited it before him (Fig. 15). At the end of his journey, he observed: 'It is not easy to be the first Englishman nowadays';[58] a comment underscored by his sense of quiet pride in this achievement which had followed only four years after another even more remarkable 'first': his successful crossing of Aussa to the end of the Awash River in Ethiopia. After submitting his official report in 1939, Thesiger described his experiences in a detailed article, 'A Camel Journey to Tibesti', printed in the *Geographical Journal*. This was followed by other accounts in *Arabian Sands* (1959), *Desert, Marsh and Mountain* (1979) and *The Life of My Choice* (1987).

FIG.15 Wilfred Thesiger's expedition party in the volcanic terrain of the Tibesti Mountains. *Tibesti, Chad. 1938.*

From the Sudan's western border, Thesiger's small party travelled through Oudai, along the west flank of the Ennedi Mountains to Fada; and from there, touching the Ouaita, Oude and Moussu oases, to Faya in Borkou. Although it has no pretensions to literary style, Thesiger's

itinerary, taken from his previously unpublished report, is nevertheless indispensable as a guide for those who might wish to trace his route as accurately as possible on a map:

> The country through which I passed was as follows. From Tini, on the Sudan frontier, through Northern Wadai to Burba, the Wadi Arno and Bagussi wells to the Wadi Haouach . . . Thence I marched along the Western edge of the plateau of Ennedi to Fada. The name Ennedi is known to the *nas* [*nas el-khala* – 'men of the desert' and by inference, nomads] who call this area by a number of local names, such as Muno, by which name they know the plateaux to the west of Ito. From Fada I went to Faya, by the wells of Oum el Adam, more usually known as Oueita, Oude, marked Oueita on the map, and Moussou. I then went to Gouro, and thence to Modiounga and up on to the summit of Emi Koussi. I next crossed into the valley of the Miski at Beni Herdi, followed this valley up to the Modra, passed over the pass of Modra into the Zoumorie and followed this down to Bardai. From Bardai I visited Aouzou, and also the Trou au Natron known to the Tibbu [tribe] as Doon. Having returned to Bardai I went to Zouar, by the hot springs of Soboron and the Gorge of Forchi. From Zouar I returned to Faya by Sherda, Oudigue, the lower Miski, Tire Tigui and Bedo. I then went to Ouinanga Kebir, Ouinanga Saghir and Dimi returning to Fada by the Wadi N'Kaola and Kika. From Fada I was obliged owing to lack of time to return to Tini by very much the same route as I had taken on the way up.[59]

Thesiger's map of Tibesti and its surroundings – which he took with him on his journey – was the 1933 edition of Lieutenant-Colonel Tilho's survey, printed in Paris by the Service Géographique de l'Armée. The map had been cut up into small sections, mounted on a folded linen sheet for extra durability. Most of Thesiger's maps were reinforced in the same way. Thesiger evidently took great care of them. The Tibesti map is to this day in remarkably good condition after being carried in a saddle-bag for 2,000 miles across the Sahara and unfolded and refolded by Thesiger many times during his journey. At Bardai in Tibesti he photographed and sketched petroglyphs of human figures and

FIG.16 Rock art in northern Tibesti: 'On my way back to Bardai I copied a number of petroglyphs. Some were hammered, others chiselled, as much as half an inch deep in the hard rock. The largest, of a cow, was eleven feet long.' *Tibesti, Chad. 1938.*

animals, carved in the hard rock (Fig. 16). A. J. Arkell (1898–1980), a former Deputy Governor of Darfur and later Director of Antiquities at Khartoum, enthused about Thesiger's drawings in letters from Khartoum and Oxford, writing:

> . . . some of your pictures are most interesting and no doubt v[ery] old . . . Hammered pictures are often interesting, as being perhaps an earlier technique than painting – but not always. Your single bull from Tirenno with horns projecting forward, and those on the road from Trou to Bardai interested me very much. You will remember my suggestion in [*Sudan Notes and Records*] that this type is related to Herodotus' Garamantian cattle . . . Several of yours are interesting as apparently showing the method of stimulating the milk supply by blowing into the vagina – as practised by some Nilotics today. I have not heard of that practice from the Tibesti area, have you? Your 'hammered' elephant reminds me of some pictures I have from Fezzan . . .[60]

Thesiger underlined in soft pencil on his Tibesti map place names of special interest: Tirenno, for example – north-east of Bardai – on the Trou–Bardai road, where he photographed and sketched some of the petroglyphs that Arkell discussed with such enthusiasm. In the margin Thesiger drew the four lakes at Ounianga Kebir – Yoa, Ouma, Midji and Forodone – whose waters were coloured deep sapphire blue, deep permanganate red and deep vegetable green. The lakes named Yoa (or Yoan or Youan) and Ouma, Thesiger noted, were 'fed by numerous fresh springs' whose temperature was 30 degrees centigrade. Yoa was seventy feet deep. The water in all four of the lakes tasted of salt.[61]

Refining the detail of the lakes, in 1938–9, Thesiger changed his description of the colour of Yoa's water from sapphire to Mediterranean blue; and describing Ouma, Midji and Forodone changed a reference to them (as much for literary effect as for exactness) from 'the other lakes' to 'the strange lakes'. In 1939, Thesiger drafted the manuscript of his lecture on Tibesti to the Royal Geographical Society, with a fountain pen and ink, on sheets of foolscap paper ruled in blue. It may be assumed that this was the final version, given to the typist, since the accompanying typescript included all of Thesiger's corrections. When his writing was illegible the typist left blank spaces, later filled in by hand.[62] The scarcity of corrections suggests that, as early as the 1930s, Thesiger may have adopted a method he used in later years, when he built up his manuscripts sentence by sentence from jottings on scraps of paper that he afterwards crumpled up and threw away.[63] A former Librarian of Eton College Library recalled asking if he might retrieve some discarded fragments which Thesiger had tossed into a waste-paper basket, and how Thesiger seemed amazed that anyone should consider these worth preserving.[64]

While Thesiger rarely photographed people or animals in rapid movement, in the Sudan he took evocative pictures of Nuer and Dinka people dancing; Nuer staging mock-fights; and Nuba wrestlers at a funeral ceremony in Kordofan, capturing perfectly the struggle between village champions, locked head-to-head in their ritual combat (Fig. 17 overleaf). In 1949, two years after he co-founded the Magnum photographic agency, George Roger visited Kordofan where he photographed Kao-Nyaro bracelet-fighters and Korongo wrestlers. His famous picture of a champion wrestler being carried shoulder-high inspired the German film-maker Leni Riefenstahl to return year after year to the Nuba Hills. Her sojourns among the Nuba were documented in two beautifully illustrated books, *The Last of the Nuba* (1972) and *The People of Kau* (1976).

Thesiger was fiercely critical of Riefenstahl, claiming she paid extravagant sums of money to Nuba youths, whose painted bodies she photographed in almost forensic detail. In 1992 Thesiger said: 'The Nuba demanded the same from everyone else who went down there afterwards, and this wrecked it . . . I have never paid anyone to let me photograph them. I have never needed to do this, and I wouldn't do it, anyway.'[65]

Thesiger often remarked how much he would have liked to go on serving in Northern Darfur where he found peace and inspiration in the deserts and comradeship among the Muslim cattle-owning tribes – such as the Bani Hussain and Idris Daud's Kobé-Zaghawa. When pressed, he conceded that his five years' hunting, travelling and exploring in the Sudan and Tibesti had given him more than enough material for a book. It is not quite true that Thesiger never thought of writing, nor was asked to write, a book at the time he planned a journey. Thesiger's claim held true for almost everything he wrote, and it was this principle that mattered. The only possible exception was a book he had meant to write about his Awash expedition; and it appears that he had kept very detailed journals with this book in mind. In Africa, as elsewhere, Thesiger used his diaries, notebooks and photographs to help him prepare his lectures, and write the illustrated articles based on them. During his five years in the Sudan – except for his journey to Tibesti – Thesiger never kept a diary but instead described his hunting adventures and long camel treks in Northern Darfur in the letters he wrote to his mother and his brothers.

In defence of Abyssinia

In October 1935 the Italians invaded Abyssinia, deposed the Emperor
and occupied the country. Thesiger regarded this invasion as the rape
of his homeland. When he went on leave to England, he longed for his
house in Kutum in Darfur with its view to the hills across the *wadi*. He
missed Faraj Allah, his Bisharin camel, travelling with Idris among the
Zaghawa and hunting lion with the Bani Hussain. Yet, despite these happy
memories of Kutum and Northern Darfur, the threat of Italy, looming
over Abyssinia, was seldom out of Thesiger's mind. His first impulse had
been to resign from the Sudan Political Service and join the Abyssinian
resistance, but Guy Moore wisely urged him to bide his time. In 1940,
after six weeks of training, Thesiger was commissioned as a *bimbashi* in
the Sudan Defence Force (Fig. 18). Idris remained with Thesiger until
December 1940, when at his father's request he returned home to Tini.
The SDF's diarist commented that Idris the 'reprieved murderer' was

FIG.18 Officers of the
Sudan Defence Force
who trained with the
Cheshire Regiment.
Thesiger is in the
middle row, third
from right. *Khartoum,
Sudan. Photographer
unknown. 1940.*

'quite a charming chap if a shade wilful'.[66] In the months that followed, Thesiger wrote, 'I would have given much to have had Idris with me.'[67]

Thesiger had hoped to fight with the Abyssinian guerrillas but meanwhile joined the SDF's assault on border forts at Galabat and Metemma. Waiting to attack, he reflected bitterly on the Abyssinian crisis and a struggle he now regarded as a personal crusade. The Italians' cruelty to Abyssinians left him 'murderously angry', even though he confessed his feelings for Abyssinia were less passionate than they had been in the past.[68] For Thesiger the highlights of those years were his brief service with Colonel Dan Sandford's 101 Mission, which organized the Abyssinian rebels, renamed 'Patriots' by Haile Selassie; serving under Wingate; and Haile Selassie's triumphal return as Emperor to Addis Ababa in May 1941. On 22 May 1941, Thesiger and a band of Patriots captured Agibar fort and its garrison of 2,500 Italian troops. Twice already Thesiger had been recommended, unsuccessfully, for a Military Cross. For the capture of Agibar he was awarded a Distinguished Service Order (DSO). He wrote to his mother: 'I must admit I am proud to have got it . . . I know how happy it will make you.'[69]

During the war in Abyssinia, Thesiger took many photographs of the Patriots (Fig. 19), including portraits of men who had fought with him in Gojjam or had taken part in the capture of Agibar fort. But he regretted

FIG.19 Abyssinian 'Patriot' soldiers armed with captured Italian rifles. *Gojjam, Ethiopia. 1941.*

that he had taken no photographs of Wingate, which 'would have been worthwhile as a record of those years',[70] nor any real portraits of David Stirling (1915–90), with whose recently formed Special Air Service Brigade he served in North Africa from November 1942 until May 1943. In 1944, at Haile Selassie's request, Thesiger returned to Abyssinia – now known as Ethiopia – to serve as a Political Adviser to the Crown Prince, at Dessie, in the Province of Wollo. The appointment was meant to last for two years, but after only a year Thesiger decided to resign. Photography helped to distract him from a task that he found frustrating and pointless. Confined to Dessie, and unfamiliar with Wollo, at the mercy of what he perceived as an obstructive administration, Thesiger complained that he had been treated like 'the consul of a suspect power' instead of 'a trusted member' of Ethiopia's government.[71]

As well as photography (which he scarcely mentions), Thesiger found other ways of passing his time in Dessie. After he arrived there the Crown Prince had given him an Arab stallion which Thesiger rode every day, reminisent of his daily pony rides as a child at Addis Ababa. Sometimes he went out shooting snipe or duck. From June to September the daily downpours of summer rain fell from midday until the late evening. After the rain the Dessie landscape turned bright yellow with Mascal daisies. Thesiger shared his parents' love of flowers, and compared their waves of glorious colour with the brilliant profusion of anemones, poppies and tulips which he saw in Iraq and Persia after the war. In 1943 in southern Tunisia he had found seemingly lifeless desert transformed into 'one vast flowerbed' of red poppies, yellow marguerites and snow-white daisies. Describing the scene to his mother he wrote, 'You would have loved them.'[72]

When the Crown Prince refused Thesiger permission to visit Lalibela's rock-hewn churches, this was the final straw. Thousands of miles from Ethiopia, he wrote, 'tremendous events were taking place. In Europe and the Far East, great battles were being fought . . . while here was I, stuck in Dessie, achieving nothing.'[73] Thesiger's decision to quit his posting at Dessie signalled a break with the past: an Abyssinia/Ethiopia he identified with childhood, whose memory he idealized and revered as the 'shrine of my youth'.[74] This, however, did not mean that all ties with Ethiopia were broken; but rather that he viewed the the Ethiopia of the post-invasion years with a clearer, and evidently less subjective, eye.

From 1945 to 1950 Thesiger explored and travelled in Arabia, where he twice crossed the great southern desert, the Rub' al Khali or Empty Quarter, and became the first European to have seen the Umm al Samim quicksands and Liwa oasis. Between 1950 and 1958 he spent several months each year with the Marsh Arabs in southern Iraq, except for 1957 which he spent writing *Arabian Sands*. He did not return to Africa until August 1955, more than a decade after he had left Ethiopia.

Morocco

To escape the humid, oppressive, summer heat of the Iraqi marshes, Thesiger travelled between 1952 and 1956 over the mountains and high passes of Pakistan, Afghanistan and Nuristan. In 1955, when a journey in Nuristan had to be postponed, he spent two months in Morocco trekking and climbing in the High Atlas Mountains.

Hajj Thami al Glawi, whom Thesiger and his mother had met at Telouet in 1937, gave him permission to travel from one kasbah to another across his territory. At Taddert, Thesiger encountered an Oxford University expedition, whose members had come to southern Morocco to study life in Ait Arbaa, a remote Berber village. Thesiger helped them find the twenty baggage mules they needed, and agreed that one of their party could join him on his long walk across the High Atlas. A guide whom Thesiger hired at Telouet proved nervous and uncooperative, certain that he would be murdered if he strayed too far from his own country. Another guide, who replaced him, refused to go further than Zaouia Ahansal. Thesiger judged, probably correctly, that his guides did not want to get caught up in the conflict between Moroccan nationalists and the French. When Thesiger returned to Marrakech in September he found the city under curfew and heard that insurgents had killed several of the soldiers in a French military outpost at Ahermoumou, near Fez.

Writing years earlier in *The Times*, in 1937, Thesiger had described 'the resentment felt by the Moors for the French, who were competing with them on all levels, even as drivers of horse-drawn cabs in towns.'[75] He had not forgotten the desperation of tribesmen starving in the slums of Casablanca, or the rising tide of nationalism powered by Morocco's 'frustrated intelligentsia'.

Thesiger photographed the kasbahs at Ghasat and Ait Hamed. He was impressed by Ghasat (Fig. 20), where he arrived on 4 August 1955, with small fruit trees and a deep well in a courtyard with guest rooms, attached to an outer wall of the main building. From here he had a 'very attractive view of the mountains and of the village and orchards'.[76] At Ait Hamed, Khalifa Haji Umr's kasbah stood on a low hill overlooking an orchard enclosed by a stone wall. The great kasbahs at Ghasat and Ait Hamed, and Tabir Ait Zaghar's kasbah with fine, incised decorations on its walls, were among 750 photographs which Thesiger took before he returned to Casablanca in October. Even as late as 1955, he would still have been in time to meet the French painter Jacques Majorelle (1886–1962), who lived and worked in southern Morocco, which he had first visited as a convalescent in 1917. Majorelle's house at Marrakech and its beautiful garden became tourist attractions, with tiled steps and walls of Majorelle blue – a pigment used by the Berbers and named by Europeans after him. Majorelle's figure studies were

FIG. 20 Kasbahs at Ghasat in the High Atlas Mountains. *Ghasat, Morocco. August 1955.*

painted in a distinctive *fin de siècle* Orientalist style, which was at once original and recherché.

Thesiger's photography and his travel writing also reflected an Orientalist attraction to danger, mystery, romance, exotic settings and sensual freedom. His superb photographs of the kasbahs would have appealed strongly to Jacques Majorelle, who painted many of them and in 1930 published *Les kasbahs de l'Atlas*, a portfolio containing thirty magnificent reproductions.

Thesiger's photographs of kasbahs, villages, landscapes and towns in Morocco were the product of a 'great picture-taker'[77] whose magical effects were created using the camera instead of brushes, paints and canvas. Thesiger's atmospheric photograph from 1965 of a street in Marrakech (Fig. 21) reminds us instantly of any bazaar or street scene in Cairo painted by John Frederick Lewis or David Roberts, only Thesiger has used black and white film, leaving the colours to our imagination. While it is true that the later Orientalists used cameras to record pose, lighting and detail, Majorelle would have found it ironic that Thesiger, who had a strong empathy with Orientalism, identified himself

FIG.21 A *souk*, or market, in Marrakech. *Marrakech, Morocco. 1965.*

with photography, since it was the camera's increasing precision and popularity that accelerated the decline of the Orientalist movement.

John Newbould, a botany student at Merton College, who had been Thesiger's first choice as a companion, had fallen off a cliff and fractured an arm the day after Thesiger arrived at Taddert. Instead, he took with him the Oxford expedition's zoologist, whom he criticized as dirty, unkempt and opinionated, yet who proved capable and enduring, and would later become a world authority on bird flight. The High Atlas Mountains were remote and wild, but, Thesiger felt, already spoiled by innovations, such as cars and telephone lines linking kasbahs with the towns. The mountain views were magnificent. In the villages Thesiger was welcomed, and fed on bread, honey and meat stew washed down by cups of coffee and refreshing mint tea. At Aioui, he climbed for eleven hours on high sheer cliffs made slippery by rain and abseiled part of the way down them. In the Taria gorge a raging flash-flood of muddy yellow water filled it to a depth of fifteen feet and threatened to sweep Thesiger's party to their deaths. He had warned them just in time of the danger and noted with obvious relief in his diary, 'it was well we got out when we did'.[78]

In September, after John Newbould had recovered, he and Thesiger climbed to the 13,671-foot summit of Jebel Toubkal, the highest of the Atlas Mountains. On the way, Newbould collected a large number of flowers and plants, including a new variety of carnation. Fit as he was, he found the last thousand feet hard going, whereas Thesiger, who had walked, since 1952, hundreds of miles over the high valleys and mountain passes of Chitral, Hunza and Afghanistan, 'felt . . . no effects of altitude at all'.[79]

They enjoyed themselves so much that Thesiger asked Newbould to come with him to Nuristan the following year. For various reasons this plan did not come to fruition. Meanwhile they kept in touch by letter. They met briefly in Nairobi when Thesiger first arrived there, in November 1960. From April to May 1961 they trekked for a month round the Ngorongoro Crater. From June until September 1963, Thesiger and Newbould travelled in northern Tanzania, where they walked, with donkeys, for eleven weeks, across the Maasai plains.

Winters in Morocco

Every year in January and February, from 1965 to 1969, Thesiger took his mother to Morocco. These journeys gave them as much pleasure as their first visit together there in 1937. Thesiger enjoyed his mother's company and admired her vitality. In April 1965, he wrote to a friend: 'My mother and I are back from Morocco where we had a wonderful time seeing nearly every corner of the country that was worth seeing. We covered 6,000 miles, a lot of it in the Sahara, and stayed in 20 different hotels. Not a bad effort on my mother's part now she is 85!'[80] To Thesiger's delight, his mother often said she would have been perfectly happy to spend the night sleeping on the ground beside the car.[81] During 1966 and 1967, Thesiger and his mother took Field-Marshal Sir Claude Auchinleck (1884–1981) with them on drives round the country near Marrakech. 'If you had not taken me out so often,' Auchinleck wrote in 1966 from Casablanca, 'I should have missed these delightful valleys. I am very grateful and I am very depressed at leaving Marrakech where I was very happy and untroubled. I am NOT looking forward much to England where no one seems to have time to stroll or loaf [as] I have been doing!'[82]

Thesiger spoke always with affection of Auchinleck, who had been Commander-in-Chief in the Middle East and in 1942 took personal command of the Eighth Army. Indirectly, Thesiger had owed Auchinleck his experiences in the SAS. It had been Auchinleck who first took seriously David Stirling's proposal that small, highly trained groups dropped behind enemy lines in North Africa could do crucial damage by attacking airfields.[83]

This background contrasted with an inconsequential yet unexpectedly insightful correspondence from the celebrated soldier to the great explorer. From the Hotel El Mansour Casablanca, Auchileck wrote: 'We had a very good run down here in our coach, a halt for ten minutes for a glass of beer and two very good rolls full of ham provided by the Maghreb [Hotel in Marrakech] – on YOUR suggestion! . . . It was a very great privilege and pleasure to meet your mother and yourself – a most interesting and unexpected "bonus" to my tour!'[84] Who but Auchinleck, Thesiger mused, would have written such a letter? In Morocco, Thesiger took more excellent photographs of kasbahs, landscapes, crowded

FIG.22 Celebration at the Feast of the Throne in Marrakech, with the snow-covered Atlas Mountains visible in the distance. 'To me this photograph conveys all the romance of a vanished age in Morocco,' Thesiger wrote in *Visions of a Nomad. Marrakech, Morocco. 1965.*

marketplaces, city squares and castellated towers. Unlike Freya Stark, who would focus her camera on an arch and wait for someone to pass under it – whom she then photographed – Thesiger as often as not seized the 'magic moment' almost at random. That he had an instinctive eye for composition is shown again and again by his photographs: a street scene in Marrakech; horsemen at Marrakech encircled by a crowd and with snow-capped mountains in the far distance (Fig. 22); a wide river valley with palm trees and mountains; a hill town seen from across a river; a busy market at Erfoud in the Dades Valley; people in Fez drifting through a magnificently ornate gateway.

Ethiopia revisited

In 1959 and 1960 Thesiger revisited Ethiopia, where he made two journeys, on foot and with mules. In 1959 he went south as far as the border with Kenya; from 1959 to 1960 he made a great circuit of the north.

At an audience in Addis Ababa in 1959 the Emperor welcomed him and promised him every assistance. To Thesiger's quiet satisfaction, the

Crown Prince, prompted by his father, made arrangements for him to visit Lalibela, which he had stubbornly refused to permit him to do in January 1945. The Sandfords' charming mud-walled thatched farmhouse at Mullu, where Thesiger stayed before setting off from Addis Ababa, held reminders of his visit in 1933 before he explored the Awash River. Then he had shot specimens of blue-winged geese, which he gave to the Natural History Museum in South Kensington. At Mullu and Addis Ababa he now worked for ten hours a day correcting the proofs of *Arabian Sands* for his London and New York publishers. On 6 March he wrote telling his mother that after he had checked the index he hoped to 'get away down south at the end of the month'.[85]

In February and March 1959 Thesiger stayed at his old home, the former British Legation, now the British Embassy, in Addis Ababa, as a guest of the First Secretary Philip Mansfield and Elinor, his wife. He liked the Mansfields, who had lived in the Sudan and unlike many Europeans in Ethiopia spoke fluent Amharic.[86] He was moved to be in the compound once again, where the big *shola* tree still stood by a pond near the drive, and a pepper tree outside his father's dressing-room window reminded him of a kite he had shot there with his air rifle. Thesiger's photographs showed the house very overgrown by creeper, and fir trees, many of which his father had planted, obscured the view from the garden steps. Thesiger and Philip Mansfield left Waldia near Dessie on 16 February 1959 for Lalibela with an armed escort, servants and seven mules. After marching for three days they arrived at Lalibela, a sprawling village set amidst enormous junipers, high up in the mountains. They found a weekly market in full swing, but at first Thesiger could not see any sign of the rock-hewn churches for which Lalibela is famed. These were all below ground level and were only visible from close at hand. Lalibela did not disappoint him. 'Perhaps no other place in the world,' he wrote, 'has so profoundly impressed me.'[87] The Chief Priest – no doubt forewarned by the Crown Prince's staff of their visit – invited them to pitch their tent in his compound and, during their stay, showed Thesiger and Mansfield round the churches. Thesiger photographed the Chief Priest by the entrance to the church known as Golgotha, which had been carved from the rock on which it stands. There were twelve of these churches, all of them different.

The most spectacular had been chiselled out of enormous blocks of *tufa* [a porous limestone], and separated by deep trenches from the surrounding rock. Some of the others were detached on all sides from the rock overhead; others again had been excavated into rock faces. One called Beta Medhane Alam ('The Saviour of the World') was over a hundred feet long, seventy-two wide and thirty-six high, with external and internal columns precisely aligned: another, Beta Giorgis, was in the form of a Greek cross' (Fig. 23).

Thesiger added emphatically, 'Giorgis, which stands apart from the others . . . was my favourite.'[88] He listed the churches, possibly in the order he had visited them, with a tick in biro beside each one: 'Medhane Alam, Beta Mariam, Maskal, Dairaghal, Debra Sina, Golgotha, Selassie, Markarios, Aba Lebanos, Gabriel, Emanuel, Giorgis'.[89] Thesiger's handwritten list was later kept in his copy of *Churches in Rock* (1970), Georg Gerster's monograph on the early Christian art of Ethiopia. Thesiger's interest in Lalibela's rock-hewn churches may have owed something to his father, who was interested in archaeology, and wrote an illustrated account of a church excavated in 1912, at Sellali, 'only some five hours distant'[90] from the monastery of Debra Libanos, and whose carvings,

FIG.23 The cruciform rock-hewn church of Giorgis at Lalibela, a place that Thesiger had long wanted to see. *Lalibela, Ethiopia. 1959.*

Wilfred Gilbert Thesiger felt convinced, dated the original building to the eleventh or twelfth century.[91] This ruin was contemporary with the gloomy, though strangely impressive, church of Imrahanna Krestos ('Let Christ be Our Guide'), inside a cave in a ravine, north-east of Lalibela, which predates by a hundred years Lalibela's cluster of thirteenth-century rock churches.

On the Sunday of their visit, Thesiger and Mansfield went to a service at Beta Mariam that started in moonlight and lasted for five hours until 10 a.m. The congregation remained standing throughout and leaned on armrests like crutches, for which after a while Thesiger said he felt thankful. He was easily moved by the singing of choirboys, and had felt thrilled by the 'really lovely voice' of one singer in particular.[92] When the service ended, the deacons performed a traditional slow dance to the rhythmic beating of their drums.

Leaving Soddu on 1 April, Thesiger trekked in heavy rain to Lake Margharita in the Rift Valley; then to Chenchia; and from there across the mountains to Gardula and the border with Kenya. In southern Ethiopia he found beautiful country – green and pleasant, covered with wild flowers in bloom after the rain. At one camp a lion chased and killed a mule – an event Thesiger omitted from his later account, yet which added a frisson of excitement to this otherwise uneventful journey. He determined that, in future, he would buy mules, instead of hiring them, since it had proved impossible to find muleteers who would travel any distance and, to his exasperation, their mules had to be changed at every village market.

Some of Thesiger's most striking photographs were of Konso grave monuments near Bakawli and other villages beyond Lake Ghiamo and Ghidole (Fig. 24). The villages were set among stony hills 5,000 feet high. Each village or group of houses was enclosed by a stone wall and the surrounding landscape scattered with acacias in flower and majestic euphorbias, which Thesiger's father used to compare with Judaic seven-branched candlesticks.[93] Monuments commemorating famous warriors were each flanked by carved figures, which represented the men or wild animals they had killed, as well as their wives. The figures stood about four feet in height and some were painted red. The figure of the warrior could be identified by the phallic metal ornament, known as *kalaacha*, worn prominently on the forehead.

On the way to Mega, Thesiger camped near Boran villages and drank the fresh and sour milk that formed a staple food of this tribe. After five days' march over semi-desert country he arrived at Mega. By then his heavy leather shoes were completely worn out and had to be replaced. The Vice-Consul at Mega drove Thesiger across the border to Moyale, where the District Commissioner, George Webb, asked the local cobbler to make a pair of strong *chapli* sandals by the following morning. Webb became one of Thesiger's closest friends, and for the next twenty-five years played an increasingly involved role as his literary adviser and a meticulous unofficial editor of such books as *Desert, Marsh and Mountain* (1979) and *The Life of My Choice* (1987). Togther with Val ffrench Blake, Thesiger's friend from his Eton schooldays, Webb read the first proofs of *The Marsh Arabs* and made 'many valuable suggestions' for its improvement.[94] It is a measure of Thesiger's faith in Webb's literary judgement that he had asked him for advice at this early stage, along with his trusted friends John Verney and Val ffrench Blake, whom he had known by then for almost forty years.

FIG.24 A Konso grave marked by carved wooden effigies representing the deceased, flanked by wives and killed enemies. *Ethiopia. 1959.*

FIG.25 View of the Bashilo gorge, with one of Thesiger's travelling companions in the foreground. *Bashilo, Ethiopia. 1960.*

In December 1959, two months after the delayed publication of *Arabian Sands*, Thesiger returned to Ethiopia. Having journeyed in the south, he now travelled north-west, following the course of the Blue Nile as far as Lake Tana; and from there in a clockwise arc to Gondar and the Simien Mountains. He continued by way of Lalibela and Magdala and the historic battlefield of Sagale, across Wollo and Shoa Provinces to Addis Ababa, his starting point.

Using a still slightly unfamiliar prototype Leicaflex camera, Thesiger took a series of superb photographs of people, landscapes and architecture, producing images of exceptional clarity and beauty. This visual narrative gave the flavour of his northward journey and served as an aide-mémoire that helped him to describe it twenty-five years later, in his autobiography. Thesiger's photographs recorded his caravan of baggage mules and its young muleteer; a spectacular view across the vast Bashilo gorge (Fig. 25) with a figure in the foreground; the foaming cascade of the Blue Nile at Tisisat Falls (Fig. 26); the placid landscape of Simien's northern escarpment; and Simien, seen in the distance, from above Anbasaru Mikael. Gondar he disliked on sight and

FIG.26 The Tisisat Falls on the Blue Nile soon after the river's emergence from Lake Tana. *Tisisat, Ethiopia. 1960.*

condemned its squalor of tenements, tin roofs and motor vehicles, whose exhaust fumes polluted the air. These negative impressions were to an extent redeemed by the remains of magnificent castellated fortresses built in the seventeenth century by Emperor Fasilidas after he had driven the Portuguese Jesuits from Ethiopia (Fig. 27).

Travelling south to Addis Ababa, Thesiger revisited Lalibela, where he arrived on Good Friday and attended an Easter service at Beta Mariam church which lasted until dawn. He remembered the shadowy nave, fragrant with incense, where the congregation stood as passages read from the Bible alternated with incomprehensible chants, and the pure unbroken voice of a choirboy. He found deeply moving a candlelit procession at midnight round the walls of this rock-hewn church, which he thought might symbolize a search for the body of the risen Christ.

FIG.27 One of the castellated fortresses at Gondar, which Thesiger thought showed the influence of the Portuguese. *Gondar, Ethiopia. 1960.*

FIG.28 The church of
King John at Magdala.
The metal cross on the
building was given to
the community by
Emperor John IV.
*Magdala, Ethiopia.
1960.*

Here, at the heart of this remote African kingdom, Thesiger was
always conscious of Lalibela's spiritual atmosphere. Although he
admitted he found difficulty accepting the divinity of Christ, the tran-
quillity and sense of reassurance permeating Lalibela may have helped
to inspire a prayer he wrote, that year, for young climbers training at
Ullswater, in the English Lake District. A self-confessed romantic and
traditionalist, Thesiger felt little sympathy for the architecture of his
own day, yet he had been amazed and humbled by the vision and hard
labour that had created Lalibela's churches from the living rock.
'Much of the craftsmanship was superb,' he recalled with admiration,
not least since this had been achieved using primitive tools 'in a
sparsely peopled district'.[95]

At Magdala he saw the sheer-sided mesa where British captives had
been imprisoned by Emperor Theodore II; and he climbed the flight of
stone steps where Theodore shot himself as Napier's force launched its
attack in May 1868. The tragedy of Theodore's death seemed remote
from the peaceful hamlet on top of Magdala where Thesiger watched

a man ploughing and photographed the thatched mud church of King John (Fig. 28), a typical circular building containing religious scenes painted on cloth, which was surmounted by a decorative cross which Theodore's successor, the Emperor John IV, had presented to this remote community.

A change of lens filter or perhaps filtered sunlight gave a greater contrast of cloud and sky over the plain and hills at Sagale, sixty miles north of Addis Ababa, where Thesiger photographed the battlefield. Here the armies led by Negus Mikael, father of the uncrowned emperor Lij Yasu, and the Ethiopian regent Ras Tafari had fought the decisive engagement that ended the Revolution in 1916. One of Thesiger's photographs taken from a position defended by Negus Mikael looked towards a hilltop held by the victorious Tafari (Fig. 29). Here the ground rose and fell in shallow undulations, casting thin shadows. On the hill where Negus Mikael had made his last stand, Thesiger found among clefts of rock the bones and skulls of soldiers that had lain there, undisturbed, for more than forty years.

FIG.29 Hilly terrain where the battle of Sagale was fought between Ras Tafari and Negus Mikael in 1916. In the distance is the position held by Ras Tafari, later crowned Emperor Haile Selassie, photographed from that held by the defeated Negus Mikael. *Sagale, Ethiopia. 1960.*

Before he left Sagale for Addis Ababa, Thesiger sat beside a spring, drinking coffee and eating scrambled eggs, as he reflected on what might have been the outcome had Negus Mikael defeated Ras Tafari instead.

Ras Tafari and the other Shoan leaders, if they had not been killed in the battle, would certainly have been executed. The Wollo army would have poured into Addis Ababa and pillaged the town. A bloodthirsty and vindictive Lij Yasu would have been restored as Emperor. As for what would have happened to us, with my father sheltering Ras Tafari's son in the Legation, I could only wonder.[96]

Kenya

For many years, Thesiger had wanted to visit Lake Rudolf (now Lake Turkana) and travel on foot, with baggage animals, in the former Northern Frontier District of Kenya. Thesiger's father had walked and ridden from Addis Ababa to Nairobi in 1913–14 and had written letters to Wilfred illustrated with vivid sketches of big game. Since those days Thesiger had longed to see the country for himself, its nomadic tribes and its wildlife; not least the jade-green lake, discovered in 1888 by Count Sámuel Teleki von Szék (1845–1916) and his companion Lieutenant Ludwig von Höhnel (1857–1942). Von Höhnel's two-volume account of the expedition was a work which Thesiger acquired much later, along with Arthur H. Neumann's *Elephant-Hunting in East Equatorial Africa* (1898) and Donaldson Smith's *Through Unknown African Countries* (1897). Letters he wrote to his mother from school would sometimes include a list of books he wanted her to buy. From his brother Brian he got C. H. Stigand's *To Abyssinia through an Unknown Land* (1910), which their nurse Minna Buckle had owned, then passed on to Brian. For his fourteenth birthday, Wilfred's mother gave him *The Ivory Raiders* (1923) by Major Henry Rayne, whose book *Sun, Sand and Somals* (1921) he added in due course to his growing African collection.

Apart from Lake Rudolf, Thesiger's journeys in northern Kenya were made without any definite geographical objective. Year after year, he crossed the same territory with a few tribesmen and camels, continually on the move for eight or nine months. He had felt certain that after a year or two he would have seen as much as he wanted of this country; but the tribes, animals and semi-desert of the Northern Frontier District proved an irresistible attraction. Instead, Thesiger spent much of the next thirty-five years travelling, and eventually living, among the beautiful equatorial settings of what is known as Kenya's Eastern Rift Valley Province.

Thesiger set out on his first long foot-safari to Lake Rudolf from Kula Mawe near Isiolo. George Webb had introduced him to the Governor of Kenya, Sir Patrick Renison, who gave Thesiger and his companion, Frank Steele, permission to travel anywhere they wished in the Northern Frontier District. Thesiger and Steele had met in 1952 in Basra, where Steele served as Vice-Consul; and, from time to time, Steele joined Thesiger, for a few days, in the Iraqi marshes. Before he came to Iraq, Steele had worked as a District Officer in Uganda and hunted big game fairly extensively, including marauding elephant and lion. He noted that despite Thesiger's experience of big game hunting in the Sudan he seemed nervous, at first, approaching elephant and rhinoceros. Thesiger denied this:

> I wasn't afraid. I'd shot four elephant [in the southern Sudan]; and I'd seen one white rhino. All that happened more than twenty years before I'd first travelled in Kenya. I suppose it took me some time to get accustomed to travelling in country where you never knew what to expect, and whether you'd walk round a bush and come face to face with an elephant or a gazelle. That, of course, was the attraction. That, and the deserts up north and the nomadic tribes, the Turkana and the Rendille, who lived there.[97]

Archer's Post, four days' march from Kula Mawe, reminded him of the 'kindly giant' Sir Geoffrey Archer (1882–1964), the African administrator after whom it was named. Thesiger and Steele crossed the Milgis, a dry watercourse separating the Mathews Range and Ndoto Mountains. The author and biologist John Hillaby followed this route in 1963 and wrote to Thesiger, 'that prince of modern travellers',[98] that 'There was nothing very original [in this] but you must understand it was a city type's first go'.[99] Looking northward from the Ndoto

Mountains, to Thesiger's undisguised relief, 'there was nothing ahead of us but desert country to the Ethiopian frontier and far beyond. This gave me the satisfaction of knowing that all the farms, ranches and towns were far behind and that ahead of us were only scattered wells, the encampments of nomads and wild animals.'[100]

Until South Horr, Thesiger and Steele had travelled through Samburu country, where Thesiger photographed these tall, 'strikingly handsome' kinsmen of the Maasai.[101] At Kurungu he found wonderful subjects among the Turkana, graceful young men with classical features, some herding goats, others filling their calabashes with water. In contrast with the heavier-bodied Nuba of the Sudan, the Samburu and Turkana matched his ideal of a slender, sculpted physique.

After an exhausting trek from South Horr, for two days over a water-less chaos of red and black lava boulders, suddenly Lake Rudolf was below them stretching towards Ethiopia in the far distance. In *My Kenya Days* (1994) Thesiger wrote, 'Few other sights have made a greater impact on me.'[102] Lake Rudolf had been their main objective. Having achieved it, Thesiger barely suggests the thrill this gave him, just as he wrote sparingly of his discovery of the Awash River's end, and his crossings of the Empty Quarter in Arabia. Instead, he imagined what 'this sight must have meant to Teleki and Von Höhnel in 1888, as they stood, surrounded by their valiant but exhausted porters, having at last reached this hitherto unknown lake, after their long and perilous journey from the coast'.[103]

From Lake Rudolf they circled Mount Kulal, and crossed the Chalbi Desert to Marsabit whose forest-clad slopes, half-obscured by cloud, rose from a scorched wilderness, wasted by drought. At waterholes Thesiger saw Rendille tribesmen and their camels, the men naked to the waist and armed with spears. At Marsabit, to Thesiger's regret, Frank Steele left for England. Thesiger trekked from Marsabit to Lodwar and Baragoi, south to Lake Baringo where he camped, and from Baringo north-east to Maralal. This was his first visit to the small township 7,000 feet up on the Lorogi Plateau where so much of his later life in Kenya was destined to be spent.

In April 1961 Thesiger drove from Nairobi to Ngorongoro, Tanzania (known until 1964 as Tanganyika), where John Newbould now worked as a Pasture Research Officer. His house overlooked the vast crater where herds of antelope and other big game roamed on a green, grassy plain 2,000 feet below. Thesiger and Newbould walked for a month round the crater, with donkeys they had hired from some Maasai (Fig. 30). Thesiger photographed the Maasai, whom he thought 'incredibly beautiful'.[104] They wore only a piece of cloth over one shoulder and carried long-bladed, heavy spears. Newbould later begged Thesiger to send him some prints, adding 'I prefer pictures of Masai to landscape and game. I quite often meet people whom you photographed, and they ask to see their pictures.'[105] Newbould wrote:

> Since you left I have got to know the Masai very much better . . . I have taken to doing foot safaris, carrying only a blanket and sleeping in Masai *bomas*. They are in fact very comfortable, and at high altitudes very much warmer than a tent. The Masai are hospitable and good company, although I get fed up with their interminable wranglings and arguments going on until 3 or 4 am on a night when I am dead tired. But it is quite an amusing way of travelling and I cannot think why we did not try something like it . . .[106]

The more Thesiger saw of the Maasai, the more he liked them. Yet he feared what the tribesmen's future had in store. 'They have scorned everything which the west has offered them,' he wrote, 'and how right they are. The tragedy is that others who have not . . . are bound to win in the modern world, though they lose their souls in the process.'[107]

FIG.30 On safari with donkeys around the Ngorongoro Crater. *Ngorongoro, Tanzania. 1961.*

Thirty years later, at Maralal, he would have reason to reflect upon this sadly prophetic observation.

In February 1962, accompanied by George Webb, Thesiger climbed to the summit of Mount Kilimanjaro. Back in northern Kenya, he trekked with camels from Garba Tula to Lake Rudolf. After that, he travelled by canoe down the Tana River as far as Walu, then walked for five days with donkeys to Lamu on the coast. In August, Thesiger rejoined Newbould at Ngorongoro, from where they visited Seronera in the Serengeti National Park and Lake Natron with its huge, noisy flocks of pelicans.

At Seronera, the following May, Thesiger and Newbould watched the annual spectacle of the wildebeest migration: hundreds of thousands of animals in a massed gathering of many smaller herds strung out for twenty miles across the plains. Thesiger saw nineteen lion trailing the wildebeest and counted several kills. At Ngorongoro there were storms of thunder and lightning and heavy downpours of rain. In the evening they sometimes heard lion roaring in the distance.

Setting out from Ngorongoro, on 21 June, Thesiger and Newbould trekked very leisurely with donkeys across the Maasai Steppe. Thesiger had worked hard at intervals during 1961–2, writing *The Marsh Arabs* (1964) in Copenhagen and in Florence. By the time they left Ngorongoro, he was longing for the 'clean space' of the African plains. Ibach, one of Thesiger's young Turkana companions, a Maasai named Olais, and five others came with them. There were fifteen donkeys, and a small black and white terrier they had bought for a shilling. They named the little dog 'Shillingi'. He was 'very attractive', loyal and yet 'independent'.[108] At night he slept beside Thesiger. Shillingi kept away the hyenas and in one camp he drove off a prowling lion.

Thesiger described the journey in *My Kenya Days* (1994): 'On the march in bush country I went ahead with the heavy rifle and John brought up the rear, sometimes a considerable distance behind. At intervals Shillingi would race up to the front to see that all was well, stay with me for a bit and then drop back again and rejoin John. Loaded donkeys travel no faster than about two miles an hour; consequently we seldom covered more than ten or twelve miles a day, since this gave the donkeys time to graze.'[109] Newbould also had a rifle, with which he shot an occasional Grant's gazelle or impala for food. Sometimes he killed guinea fowl with his shotgun for the same purpose.

FIG.31 Maasai repairing the mud cattle ramp leading down to Ngasumet well. *Ngasumet, Tanzania. August 1963.*

The Maasai at Ngorongoro had been thrilled with the photographs that Thesiger had taken of them. During his journey across the Steppe, Thesiger took many more. In 1961 the Maasai whom they encountered had at first refused to be photographed. Thesiger recalled: 'I therefore walked about, pointing my camera at nothing in an absorbed manner; after a while one of them asked if he could look through it. He did so and soon they were all looking at each other enthusiastically through the camera. After that there could be no further opposition to me doing the same . . .'[110] Some of his most interesting photographs of the Maasai during this journey were taken at Namalulu and Ngasumet (Fig. 31), where Maasai drew water from the wells, some thirty feet deep. Sloping trenches at Namalulu gave cattle access to the water. At Ngasumet three Maasai stood one above the other, drawing water in a well-shaft. They were naked, except for a leather head-covering like a helmet, which kept their long, plaited and ochred hair perfectly dry.

Thesiger had learned how to perform antiseptic, painless circumcisions, and he had operated very extensively while he was with the Marsh Arabs in Iraq. Now among the Maasai in East Africa, he photographed circumcised warriors or *moran* (Fig. 32), and made careful notes about the Maasai method of circumcision. Thesiger wrote up these notes, in London, and illustrated them with some of the photographs he had taken in 1963. He evidently attached considerable importance to them and kept them in a special envelope, titled 'Masai Method of Circumcision', which he had made and lettered. Page 1, headed 'Tanganyika 1963', consists of two photographs of Maasai, a few days after they have been circumcised, and two more photographs on the reverse side. On page 2 are brief notes, with three photographs, describing uncircumcised Samburu youths. An extract taken from this unpublished manuscript reads as follows:

Joseph Thomson's description of the surgical operation is wholly inaccurate as is that of Bagge's in the Journal of the Anthropological Society June 1904. They can neither of them have watched the operation, but must have tried to imagine it by looking at the

FIG.32 Young Maasai men not long after their circumcision. 'They now carry bows and arrows, but still wear women's dress, which they will discard after the final ceremony,' Thesiger recorded. *Ngorongoro, Tanzania. 1961.*

results. Several other authors have described it as trifling, whereas in fact the method used makes it both prolonged and agonizingly painful. The initiates are between the ages of 14 and 20; sometimes older but rarely younger. Very occasionally a boy from a family in which he is the eldest male is circumcised before the age of puberty. The initiate sits on an ox hide between his sponsor's legs and this man supports him holding the boy's legs apart with a hand on each of the boy's knees. He stares into the distance, and must neither alter his gaze nor move a muscle while he is being circumcised. He has spent the night before the operation naked in the cold outside his house, and at dawn is washed with cold water, all over his body and especially round his genitals. He may as a result be shivering violently from the cold, but he manages to control this when he sits down to be circumcised . . . After the operation the boy gets up and, folding the ox skin, on which he has been sitting, between his legs, hobbles into his hut. He is usually walking about an hour or two later. No medicine is put on the wound and bleeding is often severe; but a boy seldom dies from loss of blood.[111]

The last page of these notes is devoted to sub-incision among the Samburu and Turkana in northern Kenya, as well as navel excision practised by the Hamar Koke tribe near the former Lake Stefanie in southern Ethiopia.[112] Using W. A. Chanler's *Through Jungle and Desert* (1896) as a reference, Thesiger added that Rendille boys from the Northern Frontier District in Kenya also excised their navels. Describing Samburu circumcision ceremonies in 1976–7, Thesiger commented: 'Two different methods of circumcision were used during these ceremonies. I had previously seen one of them used by the Masai in Tanzania, and it was this method which was now used by a Masai circumcising among the Samburu.'[113] Thesiger, incidentally, was always rather sensitive about this tribal circumcision material and more than once refused to lend the photographs to an exhibition or show them to enquirers. His insistence that the notes should remain in private hands was due, he said, to the fact that he was not an anthropologist, and he had taken photographs and written detailed notes about these initiation ceremonies only as a personal record. Asked about the designs painted on Maasai shields, for instance, he would never claim more than a superficial interest; and yet

FIG.33 Maasai *moran*, or warrior, wearing the headdress made from the mane of a lion he had speared. *Simanjiro, Tanzania. 1963.*

he took some trouble to obtain the best photographs he could of Maasai carrying shields and wearing their distinctive traditional lion's mane headdress (Fig. 33). He had no objection whatsoever to his notes on Maasai or Samburu circumcision being published after his lifetime.

At an Enderobo encampment, south of Kibaya, Thesiger found people like Kalahari Bushmen with apricot-coloured skin – living on berries, wild honey and the game they shot, using bows and arrows tipped with poison. Some way beyond Kibaya, Thesiger and Newbould turned east and then north, homeward, to Arusha. Meeting the Enderobo reminded Thesiger of Laurens van der Post (1906–96), with whom he spent a fortnight in 1943 driving across northern Syria, Turkey and Iraq. It was van der Post's book about the Bushmen, *The Lost World of the Kalahari* (1958), which prompted Thesiger's comparison. In 1963, coincidentally, van der Post's wife, Ingaret Giffard, had been asked to make an abridged version (1964) of *Arabian Sands* for schools as part of Longman's 'Heritage of Literature' series. She wrote to Thesiger: 'I am so delighted because for a long time now I have been wanting to do it . . . You and I have discussed it more than once &, in consequence, I am taking your approval for granted!'[114]

Before he left for England, Thesiger decided to visit Zanzibar. He had always been curious to see the island, 'since it had been a starting point for the major nineteenth-century expeditions that explored East Africa, including those by Burton and Speke, Thomson and Teleki with whose writings [he] was familiar'.[115] Together with Ibach, his Turkana companion, Thesiger searched in the forests without success for Zanzibar's indigenous, red colobus monkeys (*Piliocolobus kirkii*). Their name, he was interested to learn, derived from the Greek *kolobos* meaning 'cut short' – a reference to the monkeys' almost non-existent thumbs. Many of his photographs from this visit show ornately carved and decorated doorways and buildings (Fig. 34) as well as boats in the harbour.

After *The Marsh Arabs* was published in 1964, Thesiger travelled in Iran with the Bakhtiari nomads, then crossed the barren Dasht-i-Lut. In 1965 he trekked a second time with baggage mules and porters throughout much of Nuristan. The civil war in Yemen occupied him for part of 1966 and 1967.

Persuaded by Frank Steele, Thesiger decided to return to Kenya in August 1968. In September, accompanied by Ibach and a young Maasai,

Fig.34 An intricately carved wooden doorway in Zanzibar, showing the long-standing Arabic influence in this part of East Africa. *Zanzibar. 1963.*

Thesiger set off from Maralal, the small town that had become a base for his long camel safaris in the Northern Frontier District. He marched fifty miles from Maralal to Baragoi; to Ilaut on the east side of the Ndoto Mountains where he hired camels from the Rendille; then across the Suguta sands south of Lake Rudolf (now Lake Turkana) to Lodwar on the Turkwel River, in the Turkana country, west of the lake. Thesiger wrote approvingly of the Samburu: 'They are very gracefully built and move superbly... They have fine features with thin noses... Most of them would make superb models for a Greek Hermes, the messenger of the gods.'[116] Thus, he defined for us his ideal of male perfection: dark skin, muscular yet slender build, a fine-boned profile more European than African – exemplified by the dark bronze castings of Donatello's *David*; long-legged Dinka or Shilluk on the Upper Nile; or the Samburu, Turkana, Rendille and Maasai in Kenya and northern Tanzania. South-west of Lake Turkana, Thesiger camped near the Kerio River, beneath large spreading acacias filled with many kinds of birds. Birdsong and the hyena's eerie howl evoked Africa for him more vividly than any other sounds. He wrote exultantly: 'I do love this life. Here one is still in the Africa of the past and the Turkana still walk about naked, in a state of political innocence.'[117]

Moving slowly along the Kerio, Thesiger sketched the simple routine of their days. They started to load the camels before sunrise. While this was being done, Ibach boiled water and made tea. After that, the camels had the hides and four poles put on which formed the baggage saddle. Thesiger continued his description:

> We usually travelled for about four hours. We could stop whenever
> it began to get unpleasantly hot and we felt inclined to do so, for
> even after the river had dried up there were wells every mile or so
> in the sandy river bed, and plenty of shade for us and food for the
> camels on either bank. Then if we felt like it we went on for another
> couple of hours in the evening.[118]

Thesiger made no secret of the fact that he now travelled mainly for pleasure and 'peace of mind'.[119] Even the anti-poaching safaris he did from 1970 to 1973, as an Honorary Game Warden for Kenya's Game Department (Fig. 35), though purposeful, lacked the gruelling hardship of his earlier life-defining journeys in Ethiopia, the Sudan, the

FIG.35 Wilfred
Thesiger and Erope,
a Turkana companion,
on safari near Chanler's
Falls. *Uaso Nyiro River,
Kenya. Photographer
unknown. 1970.*

French Sahara and Arabia. That they tended to be repetitive did not concern him; even following an almost identical route there was always something new to see, something new to experience and to remember. By then, Thesiger had almost entirely given up big game hunting. After he left the Sudan in 1939, he hunted bear and ibex in Iraqi Kurdistan and killed over a thousand wild boar during his seven years in the Iraqi marshes. In northern Kenya and Tanzania, Thesiger shot a few Grant's gazelle or Thomson's gazelle as food for his party. Once he shot a zebra to feed starving Pokot tribesmen. Looking back to the Sudan, Thesiger said: 'The fact that I shot so many lion does seem appalling . . . By the time I went to Kenya in 1960, nothing would have induced me to shoot a lion or an elephant.'[120] Earlier he had presented the skulls of the lion he shot to the Natural History Museum in South Kensington. More than sixty years later, researchers from the Field Museum in Chicago used Thesiger's 'White Nile lion series' to support a hypothesis linking them with Asiatic lion from the Gir Forest in India, and also with the extinct Pleistocene lion of Europe and North America. The forty-nine lion skulls which Thesiger gave to the Natural History Museum in 1938 and 1945 thus acquired a significance far beyond that of hunting trophies and made a definite contribution to science.

Although previously he had shown little enthusiasm for photographing animals, he occasionally took photographs of buffalo and lion in the Serengeti, or sable and roan antelope in the Shimba Hills, on the Kenyan coast south of Mombasa. In *My Kenya Days* (1994) he wrote:

Many people have expressed surprise that I did not take up animal photography. This could never have given me an equivalent tension and excitement to hunting. Although, of course, I have taken photographs of animals in Kenya, innumerable photographs have already been taken of these animals by others, most of them from cars. My main interest in photography has been portraits of people, whereas generally speaking to me one lion, elephant or buffalo looks very much like another, without the fascinating variety of a human face. I have often photographed landscapes which, after all, are the setting for my portraits of the inhabitants.[121]

Thesiger sold his big game rifles in July 1969 to the London gun-maker Rigby. The stock of his .350 Magnum had been defaced by notches he had cut in it: one for each of four elephant and twelve buffalo he had killed.[122] As an Honorary Game Warden, he borrowed rifles from the Game Department – to shoot animals for food and for protection. At Siboloi National Park, on the north-east shore of Lake Turkana, he armed himself with a rifle and sufficient ammunition in case his party was attacked by warlike Merille raiders,[123] who had been active in this area bordering the Ethiopian frontier. In 1972, when he accompanied Lord Airlie and Lord Hambleden on their safari up the east side of the Mathews Range from Lodosoit, Thesiger carried a heavy rifle that had been lent to him by René Babault, Lord Airlie's professional hunter. For as long as he continued to travel on foot, occasional encounters with big game at close quarters gave Thesiger the same excitement they had given him in the past. Years later, he recalled,

> I had become tired of seeing endless lion from cars in game parks, sometimes as many as twenty or thirty in a morning. Seeing them like this robbed them of all individuality, and indeed became a bore. This was never the case when hunting lion on foot in the Sudan, or occasionally encountering them when I travelled on foot in the N[orthern] F[rontier] D[istrict of Kenya].[124]

In Nairobi in 1969, Thesiger bought a second-hand Land Rover, which he used from then on to reach the starting points for his journeys in the Eastern Rift Valley Province (as the former Northern Frontier District was known). Four-wheel-drive vehicles, which Thesiger often referred to as 'cars',[125] had become increasingly popular. Visiting sportsmen, guided by local white hunters, had travelled for years with cars and lorries to and from northern Kenya; as early as 1924 Martin and Osa Johnson's photographic expedition to Lake Paradise, at Marsabit, used six purpose-built hunting cars and 250 porters to carry seven tons of equipment and supplies. When Thesiger and Frank Steele arrived at Lake Rudolf in 1961, they found (to Thesiger's dismay) a permanent camp built for fishermen from Nairobi; 'all pretty primitive,' Thesiger wrote, 'but quite amusing when one has got over the initial shock of finding it here'.[126]

Three years after Thesiger first visited Lake Rudolf, John Hillaby wrote *Journey to the Jade Sea* (1964), a successful book about his camel trek to the lake following a route which would become familiar to an increasing number of visitors to northern Kenya. Thesiger said: 'I still much preferred travelling with camels, but it seemed utterly ridiculous for me to go on using them, when these tourists were doing so, or else were driving up to the lake in cars.'[127]

When he returned to Ethiopia in March 1975, he spent a week driving along the Awash River to Sardo and the 'rocky and desolate' country near Tendaho.[128] In January 1977 he drove with friends to Batie on the Awash. After 1978 Thesiger settled in the first of several wooden houses, near Maralal, that he built for his Samburu and Turkana companions and their families. From then on he did no more camel journeys but continued to visit Lake Turkana at intervals, often in a vehicle driven by one of his adopted 'sons'.

Writing to his mother from Archer's Post, in December 1960, at the beginning of his first journey to Lake Rudolf, Thesiger described the rolling grassy downs and dense scrub – a country he had longed to see ever since he was a boy. 'Mountains all round on the horizon,' he wrote, 'and [Mount] Kenya in the far distance white with snow.'[129] In February 1971, accompanied by three young Turkana named Erope, Kibo and Lowassa, Thesiger made a circuit of Mount Kenya and climbed Lenana (16,355 feet), the third highest peak on the mountain, which gave him, now aged sixty, 'a personal sense of achievement'.[130] As he approached the Teleki Valley across moors made fantastic by giant groundsel and lobelia, Thesiger remembered his friend the mountaineer Eric Shipton (1907–77), who with two companions climbed to Mount Kenya's summit in 1929, thirty years after the first ascent by Sir Halford Mackinder. This reminded him in turn of Vivienne de Watteville (1900–57), who lived for two months, alone, in a hut 10,000 feet above sea level within an hour's climb of the Nithi waterfall. Thesiger had not read de Watteville's descriptions of Mount Kenya in *Speak to the Earth* (1935), but he had been greatly impressed and moved by her first book *Out in the Blue* (1927), in which Vivienne described her father's death after being mauled by a lion he had wounded, leaving her – a girl hardly out of her teens – to finish their safari. One of Vivienne de Watteville's closest friends was Olive Archer, with whom Thesiger and his parents had spent Christmas at Berbera in 1917 on their way to India. Setting off to climb Mount Kenya, in January 1929, Shipton and his companions Wyn Harris and Gustav Sommerfelt camped for the night beside Vivienne's hut, where, Shipton recalled in *Upon That Mountain* (1943), she 'welcomed us with charming hospitality, and gave us a dinner that would have done justice to any English home'.[131]

A home in Maralal

From 1978 to 1994 Thesiger lived for nine months a year near Maralal with Lawi Leboyare, a Samburu he first met at Baragoi where Lawi attended the local primary school. Whereas, in the Sudan, he had criticized Hugh Boustead and others who encouraged tribal peoples to embrace education and Western technology, at Maralal Thesiger spent considerable sums of money establishing his adopted 'sons'.

Since he first saw this small town in 1961, Maralal had been the base for Thesiger's camel journeys to Lake Turkana and other parts of the former Northern Frontier District. Maralal was the administrative headquarters of the Samburu district when Kenya was still a British colony. Two rows of eucalyptus planted along its main street were known as the 'British trees'. Thesiger first stayed there as a guest of Rodney Elliott, the Game Warden. In subsequent years he camped on the outskirts, accompanied by Lawi Leboyare and Erope, a Turkana who later joined a group of Nyoroko raiders and was killed near the Sudan border. After Erope left, Thesiger replaced him with Laputa Lekakwar, a young Samburu chosen by Lawi. A Turkana nicknamed 'Kibiriti' joined them a year later, and was absorbed into Thesiger's circle of adoptive 'families'.

After Thesiger returned to Kenya in 1978, he and Lawi Leboyare built themselves a cedar-wood house near Maralal, among hills dotted with acacias and flowering cactus (Fig. 36 overleaf). Here he lived until Lawi married. Thesiger then moved to another house he had built for Laputa and his wife Namitu on a hillside overlooking a valley, half an hour's walk from the town. The garden was hedged with aloes. In the trees were weaver-birds, doves, sunbirds and starlings. Zebras grazed close to the house at night. Buffalo, elephant and occasional lion

FIG.36 The wooden house near Maralal which Thesiger built with Lawi Leboyare. He recorded some years later: 'We built a verandah in front of the house and after that started to plant a garden. Today this garden is very colourful; the bougainvilleas especially are magnificent.' *Maralal, Kenya. 1981.*

roamed the nearby forest. Tall Samburu *moran,* cloaked in red blankets and carrying spears, strode over the hills where others herded cattle. After dark, the herdsmen sang a song known as an *ilkoronkoi* which they believed would protect their cattle from wild animals.

When Thesiger was asked why he did not live in a European-style house, with servants, he replied that he had never wanted a master and servant relationship. While he preferred to live with his adoptive 'sons', in a 'family setting', it was in his nature to dominate those around him. Thesiger reprised his boyhood role of gang-leader; yet, as *mzee juu,* or senior elder, he was also accorded paternal status by the Samburu who attached an enormous importance to the bond between father and son. Many of Thesiger's closest tribal friendships had involved some degree of obligation or mutual dependence. He had Idris Daud released from prison; rescued Salim bin Kabina and his family from poverty; established Lawi, Laputa and Kibiriti in business, built houses for them, bought cars and lorries, funded their political careers. He expected his Kenyan 'sons' to look after him in one or other of their homes and, when required, to drive him wherever he wanted to go. Thesiger assumed that they now 'identified themselves completely' with him and gave his needs priority above all others. In turn, Thesiger was faced with their incessant demands for money. To meet such demands he was obliged to sell some of his most treasured possessions. These included drawings by Tiepolo

FIG.37 Wilfred
Thesiger with Lawi
and other Samburu
companions at his
home in Maralal.
*Maralal, Kenya.
Photograph by Alistair
Morrison.*

and Lear, a fine oil-painting also by Tiepolo, a copy of the rare 1926
subscribers' edition of T. E. Lawrence's *Seven Pillars of Wisdom* and other
valuable books from his collection. Thesiger's younger brother estimated
that Wilfred spent about half a million pounds on his Samburu and
Turkana families (or his 'retainers', as he would sometimes ambiguously
refer to them).

Life with the Samburu at Maralal gave Thesiger almost everything
he wanted. He was seldom alone, though he admitted conversation was
not always very stimulating. He enjoyed watching people as they went
about their daily affairs in Maralal. A local garage proprietor, Siddiq
Bhola, was both a friend and generous host, whose compound became
a meeting point for Thesiger, his entourage and visitors. In Kenya he
felt part of the household, living among people to whom he mattered,
and who mattered greatly to him (Fig. 37). He insisted that this was
something he had never experienced to the same extent in England.
Some of the tribespeople whose traditional values he so admired

thought his rejection of technology very odd. Indeed, the traditional pastoral life that attracted Thesiger was a world from which many younger Samburu dreamed of escaping. Lawi, who respected Samburu tradition yet found Western innovations irresistible, called Thesiger 'Old Stone Age'. This appealed to Thesiger's sense of humour; and it summed up, however superficially, differences between him and Lawi, who saw himself as 'Modern Man'.

Thesiger felt bound to do whatever he could to help the young Samburu close to him survive and prosper in a changing world. Many of them were highly intelligent and lived in close harmony with their surroundings; however, few had the ability to achieve success comparable with their aspirations. On reflection, Thesiger felt that he had made their lives too easy by giving them so much money, and in doing so had raised too abruptly their levels of expectation. Instead of helping them to achieve independence as he intended, he had fostered an even more acute dependence on his generosity, which robbed them of any urgent need to work to satisfy their craving for money and possessions. Long before he left Maralal in October 1994, Thesiger had begun to wonder what many Samburu would do after their money was finished. Yet he refused to accept that his efforts to help them had been in vain. 'Their standards are different from ours. You can't begin to compare them. I was an utter fool, I suppose, but personally I don't regret any of it . . .'[132]

After his mother's death in 1973 Thesiger had regarded Maralal increasingly as his home. 'It is here,' he wrote, 'among those whose lives I share today, that I hope to end my days.'[133] Sadly this was not to be. Laputa Lekakwar, still in his early thirties, died in 1994, a year after these words were written. Six months later Lawi Leboyare, who had been Thesiger's closest companion among the Samburu, also died. Aged 84, without Lawi or Laputa to look after him, Thesiger decided, very reluctantly, to return permanently to England.

Although Thesiger's life at Maralal had become mainly sedentary, in 1983 he travelled once again with animals – in Ladakh, India, where he rode on ponies and yak from one village to another, crossing high mountain valleys and snowbound passes. In 1983 and 1984 Thesiger photographed tigers at Bandhavgarh in Bhopal. Inevitably, perhaps, Thesiger's last journeys replayed, in a minor key, the journeys he had made in his youth: driving along the Awash River in 1975; revisiting

India in the 1970s and 1980s; travelling by canoe in 1990 in the Okavango swamps in Botswana; attending the centenary celebrations at Addis Ababa in 1996 and staying as a guest of the British Ambassador in the Embassy. In 1997 he travelled to South Africa and visited Isandhlwana where, more than a century before, Zulu warriors had massacred hundreds of his grandfather's soldiers.

Thesiger's African photography

Although he occasionally photographed big game, initially Thesiger mainly took photographs of people and places as a means of recording his journeys. Photographs he took of game in Ethiopia and the Sudan, likewise, did little more than record the animals he had hunted and their settings. After shooting a buffalo, elephant or lion, he often photographed them with tribesmen grouped round. When he was photographed by Idris Daud or his Nuer interpreter, Malo, Thesiger either stood beside the animal, or sat on top of it, holding the rifle he had used to kill it (Fig. 38). Pictures of lion killed near Ain Qura in Northern Darfur included parties of Fur tribesmen armed with broad-bladed

FIG.38 Wilfred Thesiger sitting on a dead buffalo, accompanied by his Nuer porters. *Western Upper Nile, Sudan. Photograph by Idris Daud. 1938.*

spears (Fig. 39). On the Upper Nile he photographed Nuer, drenched in blood, cutting meat from the carcass of an elephant. Thesiger could hardly have failed to note some resemblance between this spectacle and a drawing of a dead elephant by *Jock of the Bushveld*'s illustrator Edmund Caldwell in Arthur H. Neumann's *Elephant-Hunting in East Equatorial Africa* (1898). (Thesiger's own copy of this rare book had been inscribed by Neumann.)

After the Second World War, Thesiger accepted as inevitable the mass rejection of atavistic values, but he did not attempt to excuse his enthusiasm for big game hunting, or deny the excitement which hunting had given him.

FIG.39 A group of Fur with a lion that Thesiger had shot to spare them from losing further livestock. *Northern Darfur, Sudan. 1935.*

Hunting dangerous game with a rifle was thrilling; whereas, hunting with a camera could never have given me the same excitement . . . The shot brought it to its climax. I shouldn't have felt this if I'd taken a photograph of an animal instead of shooting it. I'd have been left wondering if the photograph had come out, and whether or not it was any good.[134]

Aboard the paddle steamer *Kereri*, the floating headquarters which he shared in the Western Nuer with H. G. Wedderburn-Maxwell, the 42-year-old District Commissioner, Thesiger photographed his expanding collection of heads, horns, hides and tusks, assisted, in turn, by Idris or Malo (Fig. 40). Using the 35 mm Leica miniature camera he had bought in 1933, he took as many as twenty-two photographs of his big game trophies all from the same viewpoint, pre-setting the Leica so that Idris or Malo could photograph Thesiger by himself, or with one of them standing beside him. It would never have occurred to Thesiger in those days to photograph in close-up anyone with whom he was not on 'close terms'. As the *Kereri* series proves, on occasions Thesiger did take extra photographs of the same subject, even though he later maintained – snapping his fingers once, for emphasis – that he had never taken more than one. Yet another harmless exaggeration, that he had never photographed a European, was disproved by snapshots he took in the Sudan of Wedderburn-Maxwell weighing a Nile perch; George Coryton, the Provincial Governor, with a lion trophy; Charles de Bunsen, District Commissioner at Jabal Maidob; and years later, Thesiger's friend

FIG.40 Wilfred Thesiger on the *Kereri* with hunting trophies from the Western Nuer District; alongside stands his Nuer interpreter Malo. *Western Upper Nile, Sudan. Photograph by Idris Daud. 1938.*

George Webb, near the summit of Kilimanjaro. Thesiger took almost no close-up photographs in pre-war Ethiopia or the Sudan. Only in 1938, when he studied Freya Stark's photographs published that year in *Seen in the Hadhramaut,* did he begin to grasp the possibilities of camera portraiture, composition, lighting and shadow.

By now Thesiger had begun to show a talent not only for portraiture but also for capturing the sometimes elusive essence of any subject, which he called the 'magic moment'.[135] This is certainly true of the photographs that Thesiger took in the Arabian deserts from 1946 to 1950 and in the marshes of southern Iraq between 1951 and 1958 – years made memorable by his close friendships with Salim bin Kabina and Salim bin Ghabaisha in Arabia, and Sheikh Falih bin Majid and Amara bin Thuqub in Iraq. By the 1960s, close-up portraits had become a familiar hallmark of Thesiger's photography. Those he took of members of his African 'families' in Kenya, notably his Samburu adopted son, Lawi Leboyare, held a personal significance that meant as much to him as any of the photographs he had taken in Arabia and Iraq.

Descriptions of dance feature widely in Thesiger's accounts of his travels in Africa, Arabia, the Middle East and western Asia, and were also a feature of his African photography. At Addis Ababa, he had watched the Coptic priests dancing at Epiphany, a dance that H. M. Hyatt described as 'a peculiar shrugging of the shoulders and stamping of the feet'. Hyatt also noted, 'sometimes the women dance'.[136] In November 1933, in the Arussi Mountains of Ethiopia, Thesiger saw men and women dancing on their way to Sheikh Hussain, a shrine venerated by both Muslims and Christians. These Arussis mimicked animals and reminded Thesiger of the Somali dancers he had seen at Haile Selassie's coronation.[137] Thesiger noted in 1934 that Afar tribes appeared to have no interesting dances of their own and none that compared with a traditional 'Abyssinian' wedding dance or the Somali *ana-harron* or war dance. After a successful raid, Afar warriors held a dance in which two or three warriors with feathers in their hair leaped about in the middle of a circle of other warriors. Another dance comprised women, in two rows about six feet apart, who jumped up and down together chanting and clapping their hands. Thesiger confessed that he had found this performance monotonous.

He paid more attention to a *janili* dance marking the return of an Afar *balabat*, or headman, to his district. The *janili* (a man renowned as a soothsayer) stood at the centre of a circle of warriors who chanted and clapped, in varying rhythms, at intervals between the *janili*'s pronouncements. Thesiger saw 'about twenty men taking part in the dance . . . they chant and clap their hands periodically ending in a long drone. They are summoning the *janili*, who is sitting close by, and are not singing anything in particular.' Thesiger continued:

At last the *janili* joins them, entering the circle and standing on a sheepskin or pile of grass in the centre. He is covered to the eyes in a *shamma* and leans on a staff. He spits continuously. The clapping and chanting starts again but the *janili* remains silent wrapped in contemplation. Suddenly he speaks in a high singing voice and the clapping and chanting ceases abruptly commencing again immediately the *janili* stops prophesying. The *janili* seldom says more than a single short sentence, which is immediately chanted back by the surrounding circle. The dancers bend more and more forward, swaying from the knees, while the chanting and clapping gets faster and faster. They straighten up as soon as the *janili* speaks. Throughout they never move their feet or stamp the time. The Danakil who are watching join and leave the circle continuously. Sometimes one of the circle asks a question which the *janili* answers.[138]

Thesiger never heard a *janili* prophesy anything which he could not already have known or had not been 'too vague to commit him'. The Afar professed an unswerving faith in the *janilis* and would consult them before a raid or in times of drought, or after a circumcision ceremony. Ali Wali, the *balabat*'s nephew, said this dance was 'peculiar to the Asaimara and that the Adoimara have no *janilis*. I think this is however incorrect and the Debinet [tribe] round Dikil claim to have several *janilis*. Probably the Adoimara bordering on Bahdu have none.'[139]

In Wahda, southern Sudan, Thesiger photographed Nuer youths carrying spears and ambatch-wood shields dancing at a cattle camp while others gathered by a windbreak near one of the *luak*, or cattle

FIG.41 Nuer youths
dancing at a cattle
camp. *Western Upper
Nile, Sudan. 1939.*

byres (Fig. 41). Nuer dance, however, with its episodic rushing back and
forth, gesticulating and leaping, seems to have proved difficult for
Thesiger to picture successfully, as it had for Edward Evans-Pritchard
who photographed them extensively during his anthropological field-
work in the early 1930s. In Kordofan Province in northern Sudan in
1939 Thesiger witnessed the al-Liri Nuba dance in celebration of Eid.
Unlike other Nuba, the al-Liri were Muslims and wore Arab dress. Each
man fired his rifle a foot in front of his favourite girl, and over her head,
as she was dancing with him. At a Nuer marriage-dance that same year,
in contrast, all the warriors were naked except for feathers in their hair
and a few beads, including a string of 'lovely flat beads' coloured 'Eton
blue' worn across the forehead. Among the Samburu in northern Kenya
circumcision ceremonies ended with a feast, when a hundred or more
oxen were slaughtered and their meat roasted over innumerable fires.
The smoke from these fires partly obscured the scene, while vultures
circled expectantly overhead. After the feast the newly initiated *moran*
and the older generation of warriors, as well as girls from the circumcision camp and any visitors who stayed on, danced outside the camp
until sunset (Fig. 42). They then dispersed, but assembled again after
dusk and danced for hours, working themselves into a frenzy, to the
incessant trumpeting of a kudu horn. At a Rendille encampment in

Fig.42 Samburu men and women dancing. *Near Maralal, Kenya. 1982.*

northern Kenya, Thesiger watched men and women dancing together under a full moon. The scene he thought very effective 'with the herds of camels couched all round and the dancers' spears stuck upright in the ground'. He enjoyed the experience and described the dancing as 'very energetic in short bursts'.[140]

Many of Thesiger's early photographs in Ethiopia were taken with an old box-camera that had belonged to his father. In *Visions of a Nomad* (1987) Thesiger recalled that 'something went wrong with the view-finder and when the photos were printed a strip was cut off the bottom of each one.'[141] In spite of this he had found the 'big camera' was 'a lovely one to use'.[142] After the Kodak, Thesiger used four Leica 35 mm cameras: a Leica II from 1933 to 1946; a Leica IIIb from 1946 to 1955; from 1955 to 1959 a Leica M3; and a Leicaflex from 1959 until 1992. The traveller and writer Freya Stark took all her photographs with a Leica II similar to Thesiger's. She was given her Leica in 1933 and used to develop the films in her tent before sunrise. In later life Freya often spoke of this camera, with amused affection, as 'my little veteran'. Until 1950 Thesiger took all his photographs using only a standard 50 mm lens. In *Visions of a Nomad* he wrote that when he went to the Iraqi marshes he added an Elmarit 35 mm wide-angle lens and an Elmarit 90 mm portrait lens. After he began to travel in northern Kenya in 1960, he bought an Elmarit 135 mm telephoto lens in order to photograph animals. Thesiger's Leica IIIb and the Leica M3, which he bought from Sinclair's in Whitehall in January 1955, were both fitted with a Summicron 50 mm lens. In 1955 he purchased bayonet mounts for the Elmarit 35 mm and 90 mm lenses; yellow, green, orange and ultra-violet lens filters; a cable release; a tripod; a lens hood for the Summicron 50 mm lens and an Ever Ready camera case.[143]

According to Thesiger's letters to his mother, he had bought and started using a new Leicaflex in northern Kenya from November 1960. Thesiger sold this camera in 1995, including five lenses (one with a slightly damaged metal rim) and the magnifying view-finder he had used after his eyesight started to deteriorate. During his desert journeys in Arabia Thesiger had carried his camera in a goatskin bag (now in the Pitt Rivers Museum). When he first travelled in Nuristan, in 1956, he used this goatskin bag to carry spare lenses and films, but presumably carried his camera in the Ever Ready case he had bought for it the previous year.

While it is true that only three of these cameras – the 'old-fashioned' Kodak,[144] the Leica II and the Leicaflex – have a direct bearing on Thesiger's African photography, details of the Leica IIIb and Leica M3 clarify his preference for certain types of lenses and filters, and also correct the information he gave in *Visions of a Nomad*. In this book

Thesiger wrote that until 1959 he used the Leica II he had bought before going to the Sudan in 1934. Nowhere does he mention that he owned a Leica IIIb, with which he took all his photographs, from 1946 to 1950, in Arabia, besides many photographs in Iraq. Nor does he mention the Leica M3 he used in Iraq between 1955 and 1958. It seems improbable that Thesiger forgot to mention the Leica IIIb and Leica M3, which like his Leica II were operated manually, whereas the Leicaflex single-lens reflex was semi-automatic. Thesiger wrote to his mother noting the improvements in these later models, but in *Visions of a Nomad* and *A Vanished World* (2001) he apparently saw no point in differentiating between them; especially as he continued using with his new Leica M3 the same screw-on lenses (now fitted with bayonet-fixing adaptors) he had used previously with his Leica IIIb. Comparing the two types, Thesiger advised a friend: 'Start with a manual. The automatic camera gives you only what it can do.'[145]

Chapter 2

Heart of a Nomad: Wilfred Thesiger in Conversation with David Attenborough

The following interview was first broadcast on Channel 4 in August 1994. Reproduced courtesy of Icon Films.

ATTENBOROUGH: You were born in Addis Ababa, weren't you?

THESIGER: I was born in what used to be called the *tukuls* – round houses in Ethiopian style with thatched roofs (Fig. 43).

ATTENBOROUGH: And mud walls?

THESIGER: Mud walls.

ATTENBOROUGH: So you were a small white boy surrounded by this totally different culture?

THESIGER: Yes, it had no connection at all with the modern world. My parents trekked down there with camels and mules, with me sitting in front of my father. It was utterly remote.

ATTENBOROUGH: So when you got to England you found an alien world?

THESIGER: Well, before going to England – this was 1917 – we stopped off in Aden and stayed at the Residency with a General Stewart. He took us down to where the British troops were fighting against the Turks, which was exciting. And then we went on to India. I was taken on a tiger

shoot, and we rode about on elephants and stayed with the Maharajah of Jaipur and it was all wildly exciting. None of the other boys, when I got to my prep school, could conceive of it, and I in turn didn't know the conventions with which they regulated their lives. I found myself rather separate from them.

ATTENBOROUGH: And you went back, didn't you?

THESIGER: Yes. When I was 14, Ras Tafari, as he still was, was the Regent in Ethiopia and he came on a state visit to England. He asked my mother and myself to meet him. I went down and we were there, I suppose, three-quarters of an hour with him and we had some tea and the rest of it. And as I left the room, I turned to him and said, 'There's one thing I want to do more than anything in the world, sir, and that's one day to return to your country.' And he gave me that very gentle smile of his and said, 'One day you shall come as my guest.'

Well, five years later, my first year at Oxford, I found two letters waiting for me at home. One was a personal invitation (Fig. 44 overleaf) from Haile Selassie to attend his coronation, and the other was a notification that I should be attached as an Honorary Attaché to the Duke of

FIG. 43 The round huts, or *tukuls*, in the British Legation compound at Addis Ababa, where Wilfred Patrick Thesiger was born on 3 June 1910. *Addis Ababa, Ethiopia. Photograph by Wilfred Gilbert Thesiger. 1910.*

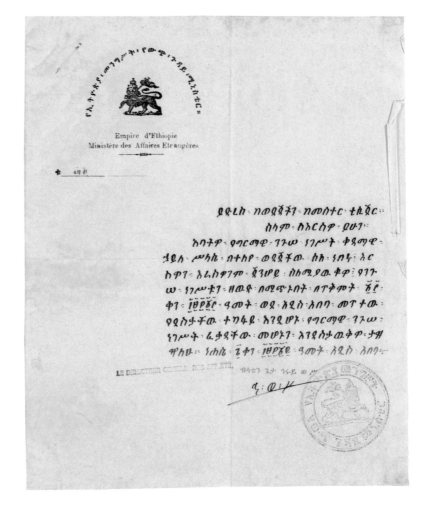

Empire d'Éthiopie
Ministère des Affaires Étrangères

Gloucester's mission that was going out for the coronation (Fig. 45).
There you are – he'd remembered that 14-year-old boy saying that he
longed to come back to his country, and he'd done that for me.

When I was a boy, I'd always wanted to hunt big game. I took a rifle
with me, and I was determined, before I came back, to go off and hunt.
As soon as the coronation was over, I decided to go down to the Danakil
country and that was dangerous. Today the Danakil are called the Afar.
In those days the only thing that mattered in their lives was the number
of men they'd killed and castrated – their whole social status depended
on it. If you saw a Danakil, you could tell in a second how many men
he'd killed. On one occasion, we were going down the path, and we
met a 15-year-old who'd just killed and mutilated somebody and he'd
put the feather in his hair and everything.

ATTENBOROUGH: And the genitals?

THESIGER: No, he hadn't got them with him. He'd killed him the day before. But there was a young chief, an 18-year-old boy (Fig. 46 overleaf), who'd only killed one man, and they were restive at having him, saying he must go off and kill some more. He went down to the nearby Somali country and came back with four more trophies and he was in. He'd arrived back the day we came to his village and there was tremendous feasting and everything going on, and I thought he was a very attractive, pleasant young lad. He came and spent a lot of his time with us in the camp, and brought us a lot of meat, and I thought he looked like an ingenuous sort of British schoolboy who'd just got his colours for cricket. And he was wearing the genitals of the men he'd castrated and I could see, yes, he'd got five. And we liked him enormously. We stayed with him two or three days. Two days after we'd left his village, he was killed himself.

ATTENBOROUGH: And was castrated?

THESIGER: Oh, presumably. There was a lot of this going on while I was there. I wanted them left alone as they were. I would have hated the idea of somebody moving in and civilizing them.

ATTENBOROUGH: And telling them to stop it?

THESIGER: Yes. It was dangerous to go down among them. I spent a month down there by myself with my own caravan. I was only 19 at the time.

FIG.46 Afar (Danakil) warriors, with young Asaimara chief Hamdo Ouga on the left. Thesiger wrote in *The Danakil Diary*: 'The thongs hanging from their daggers indicate how many men each of them had killed. Hamdo Ouga himself was killed a few days later.' *Bahdu, Ethiopia. February 1934.*

There was this big river, the Awash River, which flowed away down into the desert and never reached the sea. It was reputed to end up in the Sultanate of Aussa which no European had seen. There were forests there and lakes and mountains, and somewhere there the river ended. Well, back in the last century, Munzinger, who'd served under Gordon, had taken an Egyptian army down there which had been wiped out, absolutely to a man. I was determined to go down there and find out what did happen to this troop and get into Aussa. The next four years, while I was at Oxford, I was determined to raise money and try to get this arranged.

ATTENBOROUGH: If someone said to you, which was more important, finding out where a particular river went or going into a part of the world which people said was one of the most dangerous parts of the world, which would you prefer?

THESIGER: It was the excitement of getting down there and seeing if I could get through.

ATTENBOROUGH: Well, what actually happened? I mean, I can imagine you setting off with your guards and with camels presumably.

THESIGER: Yes.

ATTENBOROUGH: How would you know whether danger was coming? How would you know whether you were going to be attacked?

THESIGER: You wouldn't have known. I had about forty men with me (Fig. 47), but what I had also was a Somali headman called Omar. I may have been the driving force which kept that expedition going, but he was the one who negotiated with murderous tribal chieftains and ultimately with the Sultan of Aussa who had never allowed any European into Aussa but did let me go in there. I had a very dramatic meeting. It was at midnight, under the moon and he had several hundred of his people down there, all armed and lined up on either side of him. He was sitting there and we talked. He insisted on my meeting him again the next morning and eventually gave me permission to go through Aussa.

ATTENBOROUGH: You were really negotiating for your lives then?

THESIGER: Yes. The whole thing depended on what happened. In Addis Ababa at the time, the betting was that if I went into Aussa I'd never come out of it.

ATTENBOROUGH: If they had decided, 'Well, we don't want you to come', could they have attacked you there and then and killed you?

THESIGER: They could have massacred us as easily as anything, yes.

ATTENBOROUGH: So it was really a huge gamble, wasn't it?

THESIGER: Yes, I suppose so.

FIG.47 Wilfred Thesiger with members of his 1933–4 Awash expedition party. *Ethiopia. Photographer unknown. March 1934.*

Ethiopia may have whetted Thesiger's appetite for adventure, but it was in Arabia that he made his greatest journeys. For five years, between 1945 and 1950, Thesiger lived the life of a nomad among the Bedouin tribesmen. It was during this period that he made his two epic crossings of the Empty Quarter.

ATTENBOROUGH: Hardship does appeal to you as well as danger?

THESIGER: Oh, yes. When I went and lived in southern Arabia with the Bedu, I was determined that I was going to meet the hardship on equal terms with them. I wanted no concessions. I suppose they lived as hard a life as any people – possibly the Bushmen are harder. But I was with them for five years, and during that time, you always had the dull ache of hunger – you gorged for two days if they killed a young camel. And there was a nagging thirst.

These sand dunes were 700 feet high; 700 hundred feet of wind-blown sand, like mountains. The problem was to get the camels over the dunes. The crisis came when we had to get from one well to the other, which took us fourteen days. We were rationed to one pint of water a day and the temperature was fairly high. You had to climb these sand dunes and spent all day longing for your mug of water in the evening. And then, when we finally got to the well, we'd completely run out of food, and for four days we had absolutely nothing to eat, which was an interesting experience, but not one I want to repeat.

Then there was always the risk of being shot. When you saw people in the distance – our rifles were right in our hands – you'd fire some shots over their heads to see if they were friendly or not. If they were, they threw up sand – that indicated that they were friendly.

ATTENBOROUGH: What if you'd got a bullet back?

THESIGER: Oh, then there would have been fighting. When I did my second crossing of the Empty Quarter, they said, 'This is madness, you'll be killed. As soon as you cross the sand and you get into the other people's territory, they'll kill you.' And I thought that, if they heard I was a Christian, they probably wouldn't kill us, they'd take us to Ibn Saud. In point of fact, I was wrong and they certainly would have killed us.

ATTENBOROUGH: You travelled in many parts of the world where the fact that you were a Christian would have been a reason for hating you.

THESIGER: Yes, that happened the second time we crossed the Empty Quarter and went into Saudi Arabia. The last of the Akhwan – a very religious brotherhood – they hated me. They said, 'Why do you bring this Christian here to defile our land?' And when we were finally leaving them, we'd got an eight-day journey ahead of us, but I didn't know the country, nor did the other four. We tried to get a guide, but they said, 'Give you a guide? No, go off and die in the desert – we hope you do. And don't come back here.' And they spat on the ground when I went past. I had met – for the first time – real fanaticism. Very unpleasant.

ATTENBOROUGH: Are you, in fact, a believing Christian?

THESIGER: Well, nominally.

ATTENBOROUGH: But if you are – if you are only nominally – might you not have considered becoming a Muslim?

THESIGER: No, never.

ATTENBOROUGH: Why?

THESIGER: Well, family pride, I think. My family weren't Muslims, and I wasn't going to become a Muslim.

ATTENBOROUGH: What you're describing is very alien to most people these days. I mean, the alternative view would be, 'Well, any fool can be uncomfortable.' How would you refute that particular line?

THESIGER: I'm not a masochist, but I wanted to live as these people lived. I wanted to be one of them, I wanted to be accepted by them, and if I'd gone down there and had taken special food and stuff myself, they wouldn't have gone with me. I dressed as they were. For five years, I walked bare-footed, and in so far as I could, I identified myself with them.

ATTENBOROUGH: If you look back over your life up to then, you had done some very tough things. You had been a boxing blue at Oxford, taking quite a lot of punishment, I imagine.

THESIGER: Yes. I got my nose broken and my ear cut. I was in a mess, but anyway I'd just won the fight.

ATTENBOROUGH: And then, for your holidays, you elected to go as a deckhand on a Hull trawler. That couldn't have been comfortable.

THESIGER: No, that's the hardest work I've ever done. I spent a month doing that.

ATTENBOROUGH: But you were doing that for fun. I mean, you were doing that because you wished to.

THESIGER: Yes. There was no compulsion. Somebody said to me when I climbed on board, 'Anybody who comes trawling for pleasure ought to go to hell for a pastime.' I almost felt that that was justified before I'd finished.

ATTENBOROUGH: Would you go to hell for a pastime?

THESIGER: No, certainly not.

ATTENBOROUGH: Do you think that hardship and, indeed, suffering bring nobility?

THESIGER: I think the harder the life, the finer the type, yes, and I certainly felt this about the Bedu. When I went there, I felt that the difficulty was going to be living up physically to the hardships of their life. But, on the contrary, it was the difficulty of meeting their high standards: their generosity, their patience, their loyalty, their courage and all these things. And they had a quality of nobility. I've met noble people, but you can't generally say that the British or the French as societies are noble – they're not. But this tribe was. It was almost universal. And everything that happened in that tribe was known. Somebody might be 300 miles away, but sooner or later, they'd meet up with the others, and if somebody had distinguished himself, fighting or whatever it was, the word would get about. If, and it was rare, somebody had behaved disgracefully, again that would be heard, and then they'd say, 'God blacken the face of so and so.'

Throughout his Arabian journeys, Thesiger travelled with two young Bedouin of the Rashid tribe. Their names were Salim bin Kabina and Salim bin Ghabaisha.

ATTENBOROUGH: How did you meet these two 16-year-old lads?

THESIGER: Well, one of them – bin Kabina – went on my first journey. He just turned up. He wanted to come with us, and I said, 'All right, go off and get a camel and a rifle and come.' He stayed with me for five years. When I came back after my first journey, bin Kabina said, 'I want to take Salim bin Ghabaisha. He's a great friend of mine. The two of us will always be with you', which they were.

ATTENBOROUGH: So overnight, these two 16-year-olds decided that they would give you their loyalty to the point of death?

THESIGER: Well, not to start with, but they came along with me, and then we did have this very close relationship.

ATTENBOROUGH: But if you had met somebody else, the code of the desert was such, was it not, that you either fought them or they became your total friend to the extent that you shared everything with them?

THESIGER: If you were travelling, somebody you didn't even know might join up with you, in order to use your water and your food. Then, if he was attacked, because he was your travelling companion you had to die in his defence.

ATTENBOROUGH: You may not have known him for more than a day?

THESIGER: No, you mightn't have known him for more than a day or two, but if he was actually travelling with you, then you had this sacred bond.

ATTENBOROUGH: And that was noble, was it?

THESIGER: Well, I think it was, yes.

ATTENBOROUGH: You describe being very close to starvation. Did you then share food?

THESIGER: Oh, yes. On one occasion, we hadn't touched meat for days, and one of my companions jumped off his camel, having seen where a hare had gone into a bush. Anyway he caught that hare. This was in the morning. We talked about nothing else. How we were going to cook it. How we were going to eat it. One of them said, 'We'll roast it.' The other said, 'No, I'm damned if we're going to roast it. We're going to have soup. Even if we run short of water, we're going to have soup tonight.'

And then he was sitting there cooking it in the evening, and I said, 'Is it ready yet?' and he said, 'No, give it another minute or two.' And then he looked up, and he said, 'Oh God', and there, coming across the dunes towards us, were three Arabs. So we stood up and we made them welcome, and we said that God had brought them, and that they were a thousand times welcome. And then bin Kabina made them some coffee, and there were some dates – more sand than dates by then – and he brought these and gave them to them while he finished the hare. Then he produced the hare and put it down in front of them and said, '*Dfado*' – eat, make yourself at home. And they said, 'Join us', and the others, but not me, said, 'No, no, you're our guests and you're welcome. Eat.' And so I stood there and watched them eat the hare which we'd been talking about all day. I felt quite murderous.

On another occasion, they didn't want it to be known that I was with them because there were Saudi patrols in the area. I'd had trouble with the Saudis already. We saw some tents and we swung wide of them. A man got up from the tents and ran across to us – 100 yards – and he said, 'Why are you avoiding my tents? Come and I will give you meat.' *Shaham malachum* – meat and fat – which meant he'd kill something for us. We didn't know him; he didn't know us. And so we said, 'No, we've got to go on' and so on and so forth. Then he took the rope from my camel, held it in his hand and said, 'You either come into my tent or I'm going to divorce my wife' . . . and we really felt we couldn't incur some-body's divorce! So we went over and he killed a young camel for us and we gorged for three days. But this was typical. You don't get this sort of thing here. I mean, if somebody walks past your house and you see him walking down the road just outside, you wouldn't shout to him, 'You've got to come in and have a glass of beer!'

ATTENBOROUGH: It's very extreme.

THESIGER: Of course, it's extreme, but it's very laudable.

ATTENBOROUGH: I mean, you either have that total loyalty so that you give someone your life, or else you would take their life.

THESIGER: Not necessarily. You didn't kill unnecessarily. The blood feud, which involves you and your whole family, is something which, to some extent, prevents unnecessary killing. But if anyone had killed either bin Kabina or bin Ghabaisha, I'd have joined in the hunt to follow him, and would hope that it was I who killed him.

ATTENBOROUGH: I've heard you say, and I've read in your writings, that camels are your favourite of all animals.

THESIGER: Yes. The first time I dealt with camels was when I was in the Sudan.

ATTENBOROUGH: A lot of people tend to think that camels are recalcitrant, bad-tempered, spitting, not the most attractive of animals.

THESIGER: Our lives depended on our camels. Individual camels, I had an enormous admiration for them. The Arabs call them God's gift: '*Ata Allah*'. What's so splendid and marvellous about them is their patience, what they put up with. Anybody who looks at the photographs in my book will see there was really nothing for the camels to eat. They somehow managed. A camel is meant to go sixteen days walking over these dunes without a drink. And they did it. You see in one photograph (Fig. 48) bin Kabina advancing with two little tufts of stuff in his hand – he had climbed right up a dune just to get those for his camel.

FIG.48 Sand dunes in the Empty Quarter of southern Arabia, with Thesiger's travelling companion Salim bin Kabina carrying fodder for his camel. *Empty Quarter, Saudi Arabia. 1948.*

ATTENBOROUGH: At other times in your life, of course, you lived, as you live now, in Kenya, and have seen lots of other kinds of animals. What do you think is the most dangerous animal in Africa?

THESIGER: I think, probably, a rhino is the most unpredictable. I'd be doing these patrols with perhaps eight or ten game scouts, and if they saw elephant, they'd say, 'Elephant' or 'Lion' or 'Buffalo', but if anybody mentioned the word '*Faro*', which means a rhinoceros, everybody started looking for a tree. But if you're actually hunting, then you can dispute whether it's the buffalo or lion. I think lion are the most dangerous.

ATTENBOROUGH: Do you?

THESIGER: Yes. I've been charged sixteen times by lion and knocked down once.

ATTENBOROUGH: What happened when you were knocked down?

FIG.49 A group of Bani Hussain gathered around a dead lion shot by Thesiger. *Northern Darfur, Sudan. 1935.*

THESIGER: I went down to the Bani Hussain country in the Sudan where there were a lot of lion (Fig. 49). We thought we heard one roaring, and I went out in the morning and there were five and I got

three of them. And then, the third day, a man came on a horse and said, 'A lion has killed the Sheikh's horse. Will you come and shoot it?' We found where it had killed the horse. We followed it and followed it, and it wasn't very difficult. There'd been heavy rain and every night I'd see its tracks. Finally we got into some very long grass. It was lying under a bush and was growling at us. And it wasn't more than, I suppose, fifteen yards from me, and so I thought, 'Well, I'd better shoot it.' I couldn't see it properly. Anyway, I fired the shot into it. The next moment it was on us. I had three Bani Hussain Baggara Arabs with me, armed with spears. One was standing there, and the lion came in low and rose up and took him. He met it on his spear, and while this was happening, I was knocked spinning into a bush. I don't know whether it was the lion that hit me or the man as he went down. And I scrambled to my feet, pushed the gun into the lion's ear and pulled the trigger. By then it had mauled all three of the Arabs.

ATTENBOROUGH: You hunted a lot. You must have killed I don't know how many lions.

THESIGER: I killed seventy lions.

ATTENBOROUGH: Seventy lions.

THESIGER: Sounds unpardonable today, absolutely unpardonable. All the same, in those days there were masses of lion and one was hunting them.

ATTENBOROUGH: You also say in your autobiography that perhaps the most thrilling quarter of an hour in your life was when you hooked your first salmon and played a salmon.

THESIGER: Yes.

ATTENBOROUGH: So the business of a life-and-death struggle is one of the great experiences of your life? I mean hunting and, putting it quite grossly, killing.

THESIGER: Yes. I mean, hunting usually does involve killing.

ATTENBOROUGH: Sanctity of life is not a proposition which you back?

THESIGER: No, I don't think I do.

FIG.50 Wilfred
Thesiger with Colonel
Gigantes, Commander
of the Greek Sacred
Squadron of the SAS,
in the Western Desert.
*Libya. Photographer
unknown. 1942.*

ATTENBOROUGH: The Buddhist view of life?

THESIGER: Oh, no, I don't go along with that.

ATTENBOROUGH: And you think it is perfectly moral to take life?

THESIGER: I'm not arguing whether it's moral or immoral. The fact is that having this urge to hunt and hunting involves killing.

ATTENBOROUGH: I suppose the most extreme form that one must think about is, of course, war, which you experienced with the Bedouin if there was a blood feud. But during the war, you also served with the SAS (Fig. 50). You must have killed people then.

THESIGER: Yes, well, it was long range with a machine gun or something. I never killed a man close, hand to hand.

ATTENBOROUGH: But you would ride into encampments of Germans.

THESIGER: Yes, at night, with our lights on. We were 400 miles behind the line, and we'd ride into a camp. They'd think we were probably one of them, but we'd suddenly rake a whole range of tents and pull out. On one occasion, we went down there and there was a sort of NAAFI tent and a lot of people talking and singing. Well, it did seem like murder, but one just raked the tent.

ATTENBOROUGH: Do you look back on it now with remorse?

THESIGER: No. I mean, you often did at the time.

ATTENBOROUGH: Do you think we in the West hold life too dear?

THESIGER: No, I don't think so for a moment, but the fact remains that, when the war came, highly civilized people were anxious to go off and kill a German.

> *Thesiger's war was fought in North Africa, but by 1950 his interests had moved from the deserts of Arabia to the marshes of southern Iraq.*
>
> *'Memories of that first visit to the Marshes have never left me . . . canoes moving in procession down a waterway, the setting sun seen crimson through the smoke of burning reedbeds, narrow waterways that wound still deeper into the Marshes . . . Stars reflected in dark water, the croaking of frogs, canoes coming home at evening, peace and continuity, the stillness of a world that never knew an engine. Once again I experienced the longing to share this life, and to be more than a mere spectator.'*
>
> From *The Marsh Arabs* (1964), p. 10.

ATTENBOROUGH: Why did you go to the marshes in the first place?

THESIGER: I went there initially with the intention of spending perhaps a month shooting wild duck, and then liked it and stayed there for seven years.

ATTENBOROUGH: What was so attractive about it?

THESIGER: Well, again, it was merely that it was untouched. It was then almost in the middle of Iraq, but nobody ever went there. Nobody'd ever lived with them in the marshes – it was a society with a culture of its own which I found fascinating.

> *Among the Marsh Arabs, Thesiger had found a second home. But never content to be a mere spectator, he involved himself totally in the lives of the people, hunting with them and, among other things, becoming a paramedic.*

THESIGER: After the war, when I went to the [Iraqi] marshes, there were enormous numbers of these very big pigs, wild boar, and they were dangerous, they killed the people. I was doing quite a lot of medical work there. I had no medical experience or qualifications, but they had no doctor in the area. I used to get sometimes as many as forty or fifty patients in a morning. I picked it up bit by bit, but the worst was taking an eye out for somebody.

ATTENBOROUGH: I beg your pardon?

THESIGER: I took somebody's eye out. Well, there was tremendous pressure and it had gone white and it was almost half coming out, and he was almost screaming with pain. So, I can't remember quite how I did it, but anyway, I got the eye out and tied up various things behind it. Then he was all right. He stopped being in pain almost as I took the eye out.

ATTENBOROUGH: Have you never been concerned about illness?

THESIGER: No, I've been very, very lucky over that. When I was in the Sudan, I had one nasty go of malaria and I remember feeling fairly ill on that occasion. Otherwise I don't think I've even had a headache.

ATTENBOROUGH: Never had a headache?

THESIGER: No, very rarely.

ATTENBOROUGH: And no 'belly palaver'?

THESIGER: Well, the odd case of a loose stomach, but that's all. Never anything more serious than that.

ATTENBOROUGH: Without water?

THESIGER: Well, when I went to a medical symposium they said that, in a temperature over ninety, you must drink a gallon a day, otherwise your stomach will pack up – it's like trying to run a car without petrol. I did get up and say that we had been reduced for sixteen days – and, on another occasion, for nineteen days – to just one pint of water a day. And somebody said, 'Well I should be interested to look at your kidneys!'

I was following the Bakhtiari on one occasion, and at lunchtime I had a pee, and I thought, 'Hello, that looks a bit odd.' I was peeing blood, and by the evening it was port wine. I was by myself, just with one other man, and I thought it was an impossibility to get out of there. I was reconciled to the fact that I'd had it, but in the morning when I had a pee, it was perfectly clear. I mentioned it to my doctor and he said, 'Oh, think of it as a nose bleed in the wrong place.' But at the time I thought that my kidneys had caught up with me and I'd had it.

ATTENBOROUGH: You dedicated your life, or spent your life, in a way which many people would find full of pain, full of hardship and lacking many of the pleasures which many people take for granted, certainly at the end of the twentieth century in this country.

THESIGER: Such as what pleasures, if I may ask you?

ATTENBOROUGH: Well, physical comfort.

THESIGER: Yes, as I've said, I set no store by . . .

ATTENBOROUGH: Food.

THESIGER: One learned to appreciate a drink of clean water, the luxury of eating meat, and then the ability, after you'd marched about for fourteen or fifteen hours, to surrender to sleep. *These* are the things.

ATTENBOROUGH: You have turned your face against family life, haven't you really?

THESIGER: Yes. I – I mean, had I got married, I could never have led the life of my choice. I should have had to live in this country and probably had a family and the question of finding the money to educate them and everything. I wanted the freedom of Bedu life. And what they valued in the desert was freedom. That was constantly, constantly what they said.

ATTENBOROUGH: Well, perhaps it might be truer to say that 'home' doesn't mean to you what it means to a lot of people. That is to say, there's an element of nomad in you.

THESIGER: Yes, I think there is. I'm perfectly prepared to move from one area, one culture to another.

ATTENBOROUGH: And material belongings?

THESIGER: No, I've very little regard for them. In Kenya, I haven't got a house. I haven't got a car. There are three houses I built for others who call themselves my family. Everything in Kenya will go into a handbag.

ATTENBOROUGH: You mention you have a family now in Kenya.

THESIGER: Well, they call themselves my family.

ATTENBOROUGH: And who are they?

THESIGER: There was a time when I had a car. I used to go to a neighbouring small town and stop there sometimes on my way going further north. There's a small school and the boys, aged anything from 7 upwards, used to come and play round the car. One little boy was rather remarkable and so I took an interest in him. I went back there one time – this was some years after I first met him – he didn't appear to be there and so I hunted round for him, couldn't find him. I said, 'Where's Lawi?' I went back to the car and Lawi was sitting in it. I said to him – he was about 10 or 11 then – 'What are you doing in the car?' He said, 'I don't know. I'm leaving school and I'm going to stay with you.' And so we drove off together and he's been with me now twenty-five years.

ATTENBOROUGH: You stayed in tents. . .

THESIGER: When I was with camels and things, I wouldn't bother to put the tent up.

ATTENBOROUGH: And now you have a house with mud walls and thatch.

THESIGER: No, it's not thatch. It's got a tin roof unfortunately (Fig. 51).

ATTENBOROUGH: What do you sleep on?

THESIGER: Oh, I've got a bed there.

ATTENBOROUGH: With springs?

THESIGER: No, I don't know what it is.

ATTENBOROUGH: But I mean – so you're sleeping on a hard surface as against a sprung surface?

THESIGER: No, I think it's made out of hide.

ATTENBOROUGH: I think that counts almost as a hard surface.

THESIGER: Yes, well, all right.

ATTENBOROUGH: And what about food?

THESIGER: I eat with them all the time and we usually have a stew made out of goat's meat, and some chapatis.

ATTENBOROUGH: Every day?

THESIGER: In the evening, yes.

ATTENBOROUGH: Every day?

THESIGER: Yes, every day, really. Yes, because they all like it and eat it.

ATTENBOROUGH: So it's quite a hard life, it's quite an ascetic life?

THESIGER: Yes, it's not self-indulgent.

ATTENBOROUGH: Do you regard self-indulgence as a vice?

THESIGER: No, I don't. But I don't think it's necessary. I'm perfectly happy.

FIG.51 Wilfred Thesiger in his house at Maralal. *Maralal, Kenya. Photograph by Adrian Arbib. January 1993.*

ATTENBOROUGH: Did you share in the traditional cultures, in the full sense, of the societies which you visited?

THESIGER: In Kenya, they have these initiation ceremonies, once every fourteen years, and the boys are circumcised. Somebody said to me while I was watching it: 'You can't begin to realize how this is the most important event in our lives. You cease to be a child, you become a warrior, then from a warrior you become an elder.' That's all important to them and it is the result of these initiations and their ceremony.

ATTENBOROUGH: Your writings now have brought you great fame and great acclaim, and you have to be numbered amongst the great travel writers of this century. How did you go about writing? Did you intend to write? Did you keep diaries?

THESIGER: I kept diaries when I travelled – for instance, in the Danakil country and again when I was travelling in Arabia – but I had absolutely no intention of ever writing a book. But people said to me after I'd done that, journeyed in the Danakil country, 'You must write a book about it', and I said, 'Nothing would induce me to write a book. I don't know how to do it.' And then again I didn't write *Arabian Sands* until more than ten years after I'd left Arabia. I had no intention at all of ever writing a book. The photographs are what helped more than anything.

> '*A cloud gathers, the rain falls, men live; the cloud disperses without rain, and men and animals die. In the deserts of southern Arabia there is no rhythm of the seasons, no rise and fall of sap, but empty wastes where only the changing temperature marks the passage of the years. It is a bitter, desiccated land which knows nothing of gentleness or ease . . . No man can live this life and emerge unchanged. He will carry, however faint, the imprint of the desert, the brand which marks the nomad; and he will have within him the yearning to return, weak or insistent according to his nature. For this cruel land can cast a spell which no temperate clime can match.*'
>
> From *Arabian Sands* (1959), p. 1.

THESIGER: I've never taken photographs with a view to publishing them. I'd go off there for nine months and just take twelve rolls of film with me. And there might be a week before I took a photograph, and then I'd suddenly think, 'That's going to make a good photograph', and

I'd take it. But people have said to me, 'How many photographs did you take to get that very good one of that man?' I'd say, 'Well, just that one photograph.' I very rarely took more than one photograph at a time.

ATTENBOROUGH: So you have no use for motor-drives?

THESIGER: No, I don't, I simply wouldn't use them. And the other advantage which I had, of course, was when I was living with the Bedu and in the marshes and even when I travelled up in the Karakoram and the Hindu Kush, I was travelling and I was with the local people and accepted by them.

ATTENBOROUGH: But they're not unaware of you either. That's the remarkable thing, one of the remarkable things about you.

THESIGER: No. There's one, to me, splendid photograph of a whole mass of Yemeni boys, all standing there, all doing different things (Fig. 52). One of them is making a joke, somebody else is doing something else. Some of them are looking at me. It's perhaps my favourite photograph.

FIG.52 Group of Yemeni boys, a photograph that Thesiger described as perhaps his favourite composition. *Qalat Razih, Yemen. 1966.*

ATTENBOROUGH: The world has changed beyond recognition in your lifetime, hasn't it?

THESIGER: Oh, it has. I mean, when I was born there were virtually no cars and no aeroplanes. That was back in 1910. They both had been invented, but they had made no real impact on the world, and look at it now.

ATTENBOROUGH: What, do you suppose, is the major loss that that has brought about in your lifetime?

THESIGER: Peace – I mean, this rushing about the whole time with these tourist packages. It's the destruction of all local cultures, local ways of life and imposing a general semi-American culture all over the world.

Naturally, in the life I lead, I hardly ever see a newspaper, and therefore I was completely out of touch with what was going on in space and these explorations of space. I was down on the shores of Lake Rudolf once, and a naked Turkana fisherman pointed up at the moon and said the *wazungu* were walking about on the moon.

ATTENBOROUGH: *Wazungu* being white men?

THESIGER: Meaning Europeans, yes. And I did hear later, I think at a mission station or something, that the Americans had got on the moon, were walking about on that, and it gave me a feeling of desecration and despair at the deadly technical ingenuity of modern man. Where is it all going to end?

ATTENBOROUGH: And the naked Turkana fisherman heard about it before you?

THESIGER: He'd heard it, yes, he'd heard about it from the mission. It was the sort of thing they would have told him. I reject almost all the manifestations of our civilization today. The only one I'm glad that I got my hands on was my camera. The photographs I've taken are perhaps my most serious possessions.

ATTENBOROUGH: And they record a life that really has now vanished?

THESIGER: Yes, historically it has. It's a life that's completely vanished.

ATTENBOROUGH: And to which you were the last witness?

THESIGER: Yes, the last witness. And that's why you said to me: 'Did I feel that I was the last of that sort of explorer?' Well, I'm the last who travelled on foot. Not because I preferred travelling with camels – I could have gone in a car. It was simply impossible to go in a car, rather than today when, inevitably, they're going to do it in cars and have aeroplane back-ups and so on, and use radio. I didn't want to be linked with a base with a radio under any circumstances.

ATTENBOROUGH: Were you, do you suppose, seeking something on the long journeys? Have you been looking for something in your life? Some kind of holy grail?

THESIGER: When I went to Arabia, there was this vast area and the sands are very beautiful. You get these huge dunes in different colours – and the silence. Silence which we've completely driven from our world, that was one of the things. And space, infinite space. The silence and beauty of the shape of the dunes. All these things had an appeal for me. But what mattered to me was the company of these particular people. I tried as far as I could to associate myself with them and be accepted by them. I was accepted by the Bedu, accepted by the marsh people, accepted in Kenya. I had no desire just to go off and have a look at places. If I go anywhere, I want to stay there. That's what I'm always telling the young people today. Don't just go touring straight across. Pick an area and stay there for a bit and get to know the people.

Chapter 3

Wilfred Thesiger: Last of the Gentleman Travellers

BENEDICT ALLEN

Travellers through the ages have recorded all manner of epoch-defining encounters between great statesmen, warlords and religious luminaries. Hands have been shaken, blows exchanged; history has been made.

The British, however, tend to reserve a special place in their hearts for one particular meeting of no historical significance whatsoever: the occasion when two minor expeditions – very different in stature yet both somehow quintessentially British – encountered each other fifty years ago in the wilds of the Hindu Kush.

Coming one way along the trail was the diplomat Hugh Carless and his friend Eric Newby, who had together embarked on a rash climbing venture in the Upper Panjshir and were now stumbling homeward, having failed to conquer the 20,000 foot peak called Mir Samir. Coming the other way: Wilfred Thesiger, his caravan winding towards them through a nameless gorge. Leading an orderly retinue of pack-horses and miscellaneous retainers was the great man himself, a formidable figure in a tweed jacket.

The Carless-Newby group was not – at least the way Newby tells the tale in his ironically entitled *A Short Walk in the Hindu Kush* (1958) – 'a particularly gay party'.[1] They had been on the march for a month, had persistent dysentery, and Newby's feet were raw because he had chosen to equip himself with brand new, and fashionably narrow, Italian boots. The shepherds they passed called the two adventurers 'dogs' because they chose to carry their own packs. Now, adding insult to injury, their amateurish outfit had chanced on someone commonly dubbed 'the greatest living explorer'. Here was the professional, the specialist – and a notoriously tough one at that. Legend had it that Thesiger had survived on only a daily pint of water when crossing the Empty Quarter.

Thesiger invited them to join him for supper, his cook duly fed them all and before long they were turning in for the night. The ground being 'like iron with sharp rocks sticking out of it', Newby and Carless – bandaged, ill, almost utterly destroyed by their perilous but valiant excursion – pulled out their air-beds and began blowing them up. 'God, you must be a couple of pansies,' muttered Thesiger, spreading himself out happily on the punishing terrain.[2]

The story is worth recalling here not because in Newby's self-deprecating hands the scene is rendered into one of the great comedic moments of travel literature – Newby setting himself up as the fall-guy to the unwitting straight-man Thesiger – but because it casts light on the enigma that was Thesiger and the peculiar species that is the British traveller.

Newby could afford to mock himself because he knew that the British would always warm to those who abandoned their comfortable existence back home and embraced danger for no very obvious reason – 'one can only use the absurdly trite phrase "the call of the wild,"' commented Evelyn Waugh.[3] But there is more. Carless and Newby had failed to climb the summit – but, as we are well aware, they only just failed. It was a hitherto unclimbed peak in lawless parts. They had undertaken their ambitious objective without recourse to a decent map and furthermore as complete novices, after only a weekend of rock-scrambling in Wales. Yet this strategy almost worked.

So what is it about the British, the likes of Thesiger, Newby, Ranulph Fiennes – or me, for that matter? Why do so many of us feel this need to head off for no very obvious reward, and without even making the job easy for ourselves? And why do so many others like reading about those who behave like this – go into any bookshop in Spain, Germany, France or the United States and you will not find either the same range or quantity of travel literature.

The easy answer is that we are a nation which has survived through foreign interaction; the desire to come to terms with alien terrain is part of the British fabric. Our forebears were traders, and with time ran the biggest empire the world has seen. We maintained that empire with the help of our public schools, which cultivated leaders and other personality types best equipped for foreign parts. However, travelling was not just an activity of the upper middle class. Thesiger was an Old Etonian, his father the son of a second baron, but Newby was a suburban boy from a mansion block in Hammersmith. Perhaps, then, our wanderlust should also be put down to our nation being so overcrowded. This little island has long since been urbanized, our countryside tamed; it is no wonder that all sorts of characters would want to break out from time to time.

It is useful to remind ourselves of these rich undercurrents, the breadth of the British travel tradition, because Thesiger, although a 'remarkable throwback to the Victorian era,'[4] as Newby put it, was at heart a traveller and not (despite his topographical surveys) an explorer – for an explorer is someone who goes with fixed purpose to record the unknown and then report back, which to my mind is quite a different thing. Neither Newby nor Thesiger originally set out to write up or photograph their travels; they went because 'a traveller's life' (the title of the Newby autobiography) somehow pleased them. It was a 'life of my choice,' wrote Thesiger – the title of his own memoir.

But where precisely should we position Thesiger in the travel-writing genre? Newby, it seems to me, represents an obvious strand in the British tradition – the amateur who packs his suitcase and leaves home with little or no preparation. He is the plucky Brit who takes on the world not because he is mentally and physically prepared but because he is not. He understands that it is not solely about the end result, but the spirit with which you go. It is the heart versus the machine – Scott of the Antarctic (and his 'manly' art of sledge-hauling) versus the methodical efficiency of Amundsen.

A second breed would be the traveller in the Byronic mould, the man – and again it *is* usually a man – of deed and intellect who goes about a higher quest (the Robert Byron, the Bruce Chatwin, the Patrick Leigh Fermor), while a third type might be termed the wandering minstrel, the poet who whimsically strolls the lanes carried by love and his dreams – best exemplified by Laurie Lee. In Wilfred Thesiger, though, we see a fourth class, now extinct. He was, put simply, the last of the great gentleman travellers, and stood alone as such in modern times. Indeed, he himself felt proud to be a relic from the Golden Age, the end point of the distinguished lineage characterized by Bertram Thomas, Harry Philby and other great Arabists.

It was a peculiar set of circumstances that allowed Thesiger to travel as Victorians had – and that gave him the impetus to sustain the rigours of such a life – beginning with his birth in a thatched hut in Addis Ababa, where his father was in charge of the British Legation. These crucial, formative years have been well chronicled by his biographer Alexander Maitland. How, dispatched back to England, he was placed in the safe-keeping of a sadistic prep school master who thrashed and fondled him. How he found comfort dreaming of the 'gorgeous barbarity' that he had left behind at his birthplace. Sustained by the exotic tales of John Buchan and Rider Haggard, he developed a quiet yearning for a sanctuary in worlds apart. Eton, he regarded more fondly – there, he later wrote, 'I learnt responsibility, the decencies of life, and standards of civilised behaviour'. However, it was while boxing at school and then Oxford that Thesiger found 'savage satisfaction' – and this satisfaction he would hope to find again in the 'clean harshness of the desert'.

We know of the sixty nomadic years that followed, and that saw in time the emergence of his invaluable photographic collection and two most valuable literary contributions: *Arabian Sands* (1959) – long regarded as a classic – and the remarkable record that is *The Marsh Arabs* (1964). But what else remains? I ask because I have written quite a few books about my own years isolated with remote people, and have often wondered what lasting influence Thesiger will have on future travellers.

This was the question foremost on my mind during my own unlikely encounter with Thesiger, which took place not in the treacherous recesses of the Hindu Kush but on a dusty hillside in Kenya, where he spent his last years before retiring to England. Although I had once attended a Travellers Club dinner in his honour, now I had deliberately sought him out. I suppose, like so many other young travellers, I wanted to bear witness to him. We would not see his like again.

As I stalked up the hill, through the thorn scrub to his shack, I remember stopping myself. Thesiger, I had been warned, could at times be prickly, and I suddenly wondered what I could even begin to ask him. His early Abyssinian treks were alone enough to make him unique among the living. So was his shooting of seventy lion in the Sudan; he once consoled himself that five lion were as much as one could expect from a single trek.

Thesiger sat outside in his tweed jacket watching my approach – those unwavering eyes regarding me from either side of that famously dominant and broken nose.

Our first time together was not, I am afraid, a success. Thesiger was perfectly courteous and welcoming, but as, side by side, we drank our tea and the zebra grazed below, it all became slightly awkward. Another young man, an altogether more pleasing and less interrogatory Old Etonian had arrived at the same time to pay homage, and Thesiger wanted to devote his attention to him instead. Perhaps I was too eager, just too obviously one more aspiring traveller seeking endorsement from him. But the years I had spent alone and isolated with various indigenous groups I had dared hope might be of interest. Apparently not. I too was uncomfortable with the modern expedition and all its intrusive paraphernalia – distress beacons, GPS, satellite phones and the like. That did not seem to strike a chord either, and he dismissed my participation in a New Guinean initiation ceremony (to record and understand a sacred ritual) as an act of betrayal of my own kind.

Nor was there to be an enriching discussion on T. E. Lawrence, James Bruce and Charles Doughty (who I knew had been early inspirations) or contemporary travel writers like Bruce Chatwin – his prose was 'ghastly, fanciful nonsense' – or Laurens van der Post, who was 'inclined to write rather too poetically'. In fact, said Thesiger, with a hint of glee I thought, 'every single writer you seem to admire I dislike'. By nightfall we had established common ground on only one thing – camels, which we both held in high regard. And it was only when I mentioned that I owned eight of them that, all of a sudden, I was invited back.

Only on my return visit, the following day, did we begin to enjoy each other's company. I asked Thesiger what he could recall of that now iconic meeting in the Hindu Kush, and what sprang to his mind were those disastrously fashionable boots. 'Acquired for the hike that they'd now just completed,' he said, thoroughly amused by the memory, 'and they still weren't properly worn in!'

Gradually, I edged the conversation towards the world at large, and the changes that had come about in the decades since he had written and photographed. 'The "changes" that you mention have been almost total,' he commented, unhappily, 'and I'm afraid I can't see much improvement in the world. Not the way things have turned out.' He paused, then added, 'But I've always been out of step with the times.' And he smiled at this – and maybe at himself.

He recalled an incident from his time in the Second World War with the newly established SAS in the Western Desert, when he conducted raids by jeep on German encampments. 'Once, while we were making our getaway, we got a puncture. All of a sudden our vehicle was at a halt, sitting there helpless. My CO said, "Right. No time to lose. Get out, Thesiger. Fix the wheel!" I turned to him and said, "I've never learnt to change a tyre – and I don't expect to begin learning now!"'

Despite my coaxing, Thesiger had little in the end to say about how he saw his travels influencing future generations. However, to me, that short wartime anecdote amply expresses his stance on the modern world. Yes, he took considerable pride in the words and images that so ably preserved his life in Arabia and Africa but his legacy was, ultimately, a personal record by someone who was not of our time – and this, to his mind, limited his relevance to the present. Furthermore, he took positive pleasure in being an anachronism. Our world would be ever more diminished, ever more insipid, and he did not want to be part of it. He was a historic fixture, and proud to be so.

There was only one other occasion when I spent very long with Wilfred Thesiger, and this time I unwittingly got my revenge on him for not listening to my own tales. I was the speaker at an Oxford University Exploration Club dinner and the poor man, instead of enjoying an evening of reminiscences at his old college, Magdalen, somehow found himself guest of honour at my event. He had to sit through forty minutes of me regaling the audience with an account of my participation in the New Guinea initiation ceremony that he had poured cold water on, years before.

But I prefer to think of Wilfred, the great 'throwback', as being still out there in Africa. As I was about to leave his shack in Maralal, he was going through some old photos. 'Sometimes people ask me where all the other pictures are,' he said cheerily. 'They think I must have edited out the poor ones. But these are all I took!' Together we sifted through the exquisite images – lost worlds of nomads standing poised in scenes of brutal majesty. Gone now the isolated lives of the Afar, the Marsh Arabs and the Bedu, 'a cheerful, courageous, dignified people whose spirit once lit the desert like a flame'.

The scene now playing out in front of me, of Thesiger looking back through time, was almost unbearably touching. An old man was reviewing his life, soon to be over – a remarkable life, and that rare thing, a life of his own choosing – and it was made all the more touching because he had to stop every once in a while and peer closer. 'My eyesight is going. Do you think they'll be able to fix it in England?' I replied that I was not sure. He put down the pictures and together we looked out over the plain. I asked him to describe what he could see. 'Almost nothing of detail. Only the odd wavering image.' The moment was all the more poignant because I had recently also had tea with the aged Laurens van der Post, born of the same vanishing era. He too had complained about his failing eyesight. Two old horses who had seen so much – and now, the fading of the light.

Before I said goodbye, Thesiger kindly wrote a few words in my notebook as a memento. 'Benedict. I was interested to meet you again and wish you had stayed longer. Wilfred Thesiger, Maralal, May 14th 1992.' As a farewell note it was a little formal and sparse, but it meant the world to me back then as a traveller in his wake – and continues to do so to this day. As I walked off down the slope I remember how empty by comparison my own journeys to the ends of the earth seemed; my life so much less lived.

I left Thesiger on his verandah looking out over the Samburu plains, and that is how I will remember him. Down slope, I paused with my notebook to capture what I could of our conversation. 'I feel so sorry for the young coming up,' I see now I quoted him as saying. 'Where will they be able to go? There's less and less difference everywhere.'

Looking back, seven years after his death, it strikes me that Wilfred Thesiger was not altogether an anachronism, not the leftover that he felt himself to be. Rather, today's travellers – if they too want to bear witness to the world – would do well to follow his lead. Living as he once did is no longer possible, but we can usefully adopt the model. We live in the Information Age, when internet cafés, mobile phones and other innovations keep us connected to our own world – and insulated from anyone else's. 'Travelling', for most of us, means a trip – Lonely Planet

Guide perhaps to hand – with those of our own culture, to sights that we are anyway already familiar with from brochures, books, friends and websites, while the word 'exploration' has been distorted to include adventurers who trek to the South Pole – though in truth they are no more than athletes on a cold race track.

Thesiger knew what most contemporary travellers apparently do not – that if you cross a desert in a Land Cruiser, or climb Everest with a satellite phone, you have diminished your experience – and any achievement. What is travel if you do not disconnect yourself, cut the umbilical cord? Nor can there be much of profundity learned if you do not allow yourself to be immersed and vulnerable, your skin and heart exposed to the searing desert.

Thesiger's legacy lies not just in the worlds he has saved for us through words and images, but in his example of how to travel. Those who are now young may never have the chance to feel 'in harmony with the past, travelling as men had travelled for untold generations across deserts',[5] but only by having the courage to let go of the familiar can we know ourselves. Ironically, Thesiger's approach is more relevant now, in our connected-up age, than ever before.

He also once wrote that 'the Arabs are a race which produces its best only under conditions of extreme hardship and deteriorates progressively as living conditions become easier'.[6] He was talking of qualities such as dignity, fellowship, humour, courage and patience. Perhaps we are all like the Arabs.

Chapter 4

Imagined Time:
Thesiger, Photography
and the Past

Elizabeth Edwards

Wilfred Thesiger's photographs in many ways defy the normal categories of analysis. It is paradoxical work. It is travel photography, but it is more than that; it is an ethnographic record, but it is perhaps less than that; it is conceived of as a 'straight' record of encounters and places, yet it transcends the descriptive to become an interpretative inscription of personal experience.

Within this, Thesiger's photographs have usually been seen as being about place – the spaces through which he travelled, the landscapes he passed through, the people he encountered – and read as records of those cultures and locations. While Thesiger's photographs are, of course, these things, in this short essay I propose a different way of thinking about them that might help to explain why they are as they are – namely as markers of time and simultaneously a projection into timelessness. I shall suggest that the photographs are not simply about time in the sense of narratives of travels, but that their style and subject matter is deeply resonant with Thesiger's own sense of imagined time, itself framed too by a sense of timelessness – the denial of the work of time.

All photography is, of course, about time. It is a commonplace that photography arrests time and fragments space, producing the stilled moment. Photographs reproduce those fragments and project them into the future. In this they repeat endlessly the moment that has only existed once – the passing moment in front of the camera: the 'there-then' is translated into the 'here-now' giving the viewer direct access to 'that which has been'. They are thus able to concentrate attention on the fleeting moment, elevating it for future contemplation. This has been the seduction of Thesiger's photographs. We can follow his journeys through his contact sheets, get a sense of the unfolding experience of landscape and people, the prints in his seventy-one albums standing for a 'fleeting immediacy of the encounter' translated into the 'stabilizing permanency of fact'.[1]

Although Thesiger returned to the African continent many times during the course of his life, in many ways sub-Saharan Africa forms the bookends of his 'photographic career'. His first photographs in Ethiopia were made with a small Kodak camera which had belonged to his father. With its limited focal range and faulty viewfinder, he began to take snapshots of his experiences – the places through which he travelled and the people he encountered. He acquired his first 35 mm Leica camera (a Leica II) while in the Sudan, but did not take the medium seriously or start to explore its narrative possibilities as a record of travel – as opposed to isolated occurrences – until his crossings of the Rub' al Khali (Empty Quarter) in the late 1940s. This caused him, in the 1950s, to expand his technical repertoire, adding an Elmarit 90 mm portrait lens and an Elmarit 35 mm wide-angle lens as his photographic interests cohered, although he still preferred to work with a standard 50 mm lens. In 1959, after his stay with the Marsh Arabs in Iraq, he changed his Leica II, followed by his Leica IIIb and Leica M3, for the newer Leicaflex. By the time he had returned to Africa to travel more extensively, and eventually to live, in the 1960s, he was a consummate photographer who had honed his skills in the visualization of landscapes and peoples, and had settled into a style of representation which was unmistakably his own, and from which he seldom departed.

Although working with a Leica camera, his photography remained largely unaffected by the shifting trends and evolving concerns in European photography. It was the 35 mm revolution after all that had contributed in part to the emergence of the mid-European Neue Sachlichkeit (New Objectivity) of the 1920s, a movement that brought shape to documentary style and revolutionary framing to interpretative photography. Likewise, there is little sense of intimacy in his photography of landscape. While he is responsive to the geometries of landscape, especially desert landscapes, and to its grandeurs, Thesiger does not see it with the modernist sensibility of, for example, Ansel Adams or Edward Weston, or the detailed caressing of rock and earth forms such as is found in the work of Minor White.

Of course, photography is many things and the work asked of it at any given historical moment is wide-ranging and various. But it is important in thinking about time to comprehend the distance between Thesiger's concept of photographic style and what was happening elsewhere. Consistent with his world view and rejection of the modern, Thesiger's photography, it can be argued, reached back to the aesthetic and representational practices of the nineteenth century rather than engage with the shifting potential of the medium in the twentieth.

I once asked him which photographers he most admired, and he answered 'none'. This was not a refutation of all photographers but simply that the photographic world was not one with which he connected, nor indeed saw the point of. Photography was, he said, merely a tool for recording the reality of his own experience. Yet his sense of landscape and environment is strangely reminiscent of that of Edward Weston, who commented that his photographs were no longer about expressing himself, but, without falsification, 'to become identified with nature . . . so that what I record is not an interpretation, my idea of what nature *should* be, but a revelation – an absolute, impersonal recognition of the significance of facts'.[2] In many ways this sense of truth and revelation through vision informs, in a very different context, Thesiger's own belief in the power of his photography to both record and reveal the authenticity of his experiences.

As I have suggested, Thesiger's visual language emerges directly from the nineteenth century. Many of his landscape photographs are framed like engravings, as found in the hunting and exploration books that shaped his youthful imagination and whetted his appetite for travel. They give a sense of majesty of landscape, of scale and the unknown. In another key paradox, they resonate not only with universal values but at the same time with his own personalized vision. Thesiger's photography does not objectify its subjects, it is a profoundly connected visualization. The intimacy is that of a traveller, anchoring the memory of place and experience through people themselves.

Thesiger thus draws on the traditional imagery of man in nature and against nature – the battle for survival in harsh terrains which he both admired and tested himself against. The isolated figure encompassed by wilderness and the inhospitality of nature is a theme that comes across repeatedly in both his photographs and his writing. It is an environment that forms the boundary between life and death, where people are bonded through the need for physical survival and their common humanity.

His engagement with landscape is profoundly romantic in the classical sense, in that it responds to the duality of nature, and humankind's relationship to it as a majestic but threatening beauty – a theme that has shaped the sublime in art and literature for over two centuries. From this duality emerges the ambiguity that symbolizes wilderness and makes it simultaneously a place of isolation and a place of reverence, of deep spiritual significance and of individual reaffirmation. Such values saturate Thesiger's photographs, from the formal, sculptural beauty of the dunes of the Rub' al Khali in Arabia, the wide-patterned, cloud-spattered skies reflected in the waters of the Iraqi marshes, to the

FIG.53 Rendille with a large herd of goats near Ilaut wells. *Ilaut, Kenya. 1961.*

massive scale of the African landscape, dwarfing people, animals and vegetation alike. The elements extracted from the landscape express a reality and experience which is no longer simply or purely descriptive but associational. Where people inhabit the landscape, they are the rightful owners and users, even within a colonial environment. They are shown, again romantically, as autochthonous people at one with their landscape.

This is suggested in a photograph of Rendille herdsmen (Fig. 53 previous page) walking out into the bush pastures with their herds. The goats and sheep make winding patterns through a landscape of massive scale. The breeze gently lifts the clothing wrapped around the herders' bodies, while the spears they carry form diagonals carefully placed within the frame, further shaping the spatial dynamic of the image. The photograph stands as a metaphor for Thesiger's view of the relations between people, animals and environment. But it also typifies his way of seeing and framing a photograph, a moment of visual epiphany suffused with a sense of the past, as his photographs perform a sense of timelessness rendered through literal and metaphorical distance.

It is perhaps in this complex relation between romantic ideal, the fascination of the 'savage', practical need and personal admiration that we must place his portrait photographs. He always valued them above his landscapes, for the encounter and experience of people was at the heart of his interest in travel. Again, the idea of time was central to his response as he sought out the unchanged and the authentic – 'to find myself among people who knew no world other than their own'.[3] At one level they are profoundly theatrical as subjects – filling the frame, people stare boldly back into the camera. Given that these are photographs of people for whom interaction with the camera was not necessarily a norm, their quiet self-possession reminds us of the paradox of the portrait, the delicate balance between the inscription of social and cultural being and an individual private self. Despite some resonance of visual equivalence between subjects, most of these photographs bear little resemblance to the 'anthropological type'. Rather, on occasion the framing and the camera angles are suggestive of society photography of the period, a merging of romanticism, quirkiness and icon.

Time is written into Thesiger's portraits in contradictory ways. First there is his method of production: he would often take three images of

a subject, pointing to the experience of the encounter in duration, while paradoxically the completed image stands for a stillness within the movement and time of travel, a sense of time on the cusp, the time of encounter compressed within the image. Even those images capturing the fleeting moment and the course of action are inflected with theatricality, created by the careful framing of the image. There is an incredible geometry contained within the photographic frame. The style of the portraits themselves, often with tight framing, play of light and low camera angle, endows subjects repeatedly with a sense of nobility. This in its turn is inflected with authenticity and time, the draped cloth or animal skin (Fig. 54), for instance, perhaps signifying the cultural values of ancient classical nobility that had framed Thesiger's traditional education. By the 1970s and 1980s his portraiture, often of friends and people from his local community around Maralal, repeatedly employs the low camera angle, which emerged for Thesiger in his photographic work in Iraq and Kurdistan, to heighten and strengthen, both literally and metaphorically, the people he so admired.

One can argue that Thesiger's perception of both landscape and people remains romantic and suffused with imagined time. Thesiger claimed that he did not romanticize;[4] however, as I have suggested, the straight forwardness of so many of his photographs belies an underlying romanticism, shaped by the subjectivity of his own experience. Thesiger's rejection of modernity, or 'civilization' as he himself would put it, constitutes what has been described by anthropologist James Clifford as an 'ethnographic pastoral', a metaphor which is particularly apposite given that so much of Thesiger's experience was with people who were, literally, economically 'pastoral'. The idea of an 'ethnographic pastoral' is strongly linked to that of 'salvage ethnography'; that is, the recording and preservation of cultures, practices, places and peoples before they 'disappear'.

The pastoral, as another anthropologist Renato Rosaldo has argued, makes possible particular and peculiar interactions and relationships of 'polite tenderness'.[5] This enables respect and admiration, while disguising the complex and often unequal cultural relations that make this possible. This complexity of relationships and the twin senses of authenticity and loss permeate Thesiger's writing and photography. For instance, while he constructed unchanging and authentic culture through his choice of regions and through his photographs, his access to 'timeless culture' was dependent on colonial infrastructures for everything from permits to 'a civilized meal' while at the same time consciously rejecting those relations. There is an irony in his constant positioning of himself as 'the first white man' to cross the Rub' al Khali in this traditional manner, or to see or undertake some cultural practice or other, yet at the same time the photographs speak to a sense of fragile purity, soon to be lost.

Photography itself becomes part of this very discourse of 'pastoral authenticity' and maintains and reinforces it in the way in which it fragments space and time, and constantly repeats and insists on the reality of 'that-which-has-been'. This temporal dynamic constitutes what Clifford has described as a 'relentless placement of others in a present becoming past'.[6] It is a position suffused with a sense of loss but at the same time the desire to define and hold the 'authentic' as a check against cultural and social fragmentation: as Thesiger himself claimed, little that he photographed could be photographed in the modern world. This sense of authenticity both presupposes, and is produced by, a present circumstance of felt inauthenticity. This complex set of relations with time – the 'relentless placement' in a 'present becoming past' – becomes the driving force behind Thesiger's photography. The still photograph not only records in detail, as an act of salvage ethnography, particulars of clothing, beadwork, hunting practices and ceremonies, but also becomes a site of contemplation and imagination where fictions of wholeness can be maintained. For, as I noted earlier in relation to distance, the photographs become sites where time and space come together and time becomes palpable – almost visible – as a sense of the past vested in people and places. To this extent his photographs stand as a form of illusionism: 'this is what you would have seen had you, like me, been there' slips into 'this is what it would have been like if I had not been there' and 'this is what one would have seen 1,000 years ago'.

Thesiger's use of black and white photography is part of this focus on the continuity of an imagined past in the present and the construction of his timeless ethnographic pastoral. He was adamantly opposed to colour photography, even when it became widely and easily available in the 1950s and 1960s. This was not merely an absorption of the socio-cultural values of black and white photography as the 'serious' and engaged photography of documentary, since it was only in the late 1970s and 1980s that colour, through photographers such as William Eggleston in the USA and a few years later Martin Parr in the UK, emerged to be taken seriously as both arts practice and social commentary. More importantly for Thesiger, his rejection of colour stood for the rejection of what he saw as a brash and destructive modernity, the superficiality of travel and tourist photography. The cultural values of black and white spoke instead of a sense of the past that appealed to both him and his readership. It was a reassurance of that illusion that things were as they had always been, while also referring back to the appearance and values of nineteenth- and early twentieth-century photography – the very tradition and history of photography itself.

Black and white photography is by its very nature an essentialist medium, expressing line, tone and texture, qualities which Thesiger himself valued.[7] But it also allows for an imaginative space around the image, rather than the distractions of colour with its stronger insistence on realism, which at the same time dramatizes its subjects in a form of heightened exoticism.[8] Thesiger's use of black and white is thus an integral part of the 'ethnographic pastoral' which so deeply informs his vision of the world. His exoticism was a profoundly grounded one, premised not in surface appearance necessarily, but in the way figures and places come to stand for all that he admired. It was through his photographs that he was able to filter those experiences, and construct a world which constituted for him the essential human values, anchored in the authenticity of the past. Thus we can understand his landscapes to be marked by the antiquity and fragile continuity of human interaction with the landscape. Buildings, such as the mud-brick kasbahs of Morocco, rise up organically from the earth, part of an organic whole carrying, in an almost Ruskinian sense, the marks of time and of successive human interaction. Other landscapes appear as untouched by human hand, standing for a longer past, a time of wholeness and purity.

In many ways Thesiger's photography shifts gear during his latter years in Kenya. The strong narrative line of travel, the sense of time mapped through meetings and departures which hitherto pattern the corpus change with his mode of interaction. The pace and tenor of his photographs alter because there is a change in the spatial and temporal dynamics of his experience. While the great sweeping landscapes and statuesque warriors filling the frames with elegant geometries remain, the photographs arguably become more clearly ethnographic in their inscription of everyday life. The framing is more casual and possibly less self-conscious, reflecting perhaps the different kind of relationship he had with his subjects. But the underlying ethos remains that of the 'ethnographic pastoral', tinged with a sense of impending loss, and the need to record before the march of civilization.

His photographs, with their insistent timelessness, are carefully and selectively blind to those elements of contemporary life that he found distasteful. His imagined Africa is untroubled by the memory of Mau-Mau, the pains and uncertainties of decolonization, the entanglement of newly independent nation-states in an increasingly global environment and emergent post-colonial political and ethnic tensions. It remains peopled by the idealized, hard, muscular, masculine 'savages' of time immemorial, acting out their nobility in harsh and unforgiving environments, as it had been in his first responses to the Afar in the 1930s. It is a vision that has its roots in the European Enlightenment, but which also encompasses the subjectivities of romanticism, the primacy of visual knowledge and the centrality of the observer in later nineteenth-century thinking.

All these ways of seeing, and their resulting visual practices, resonate through Thesiger's photography and make it complex and at times, as I have suggested, difficult to categorize. Most importantly, it is photography that, for Thesiger, locates people and places outside time to be the focus of a reverie of the authentic, the pure and the whole. This is because ultimately it is a profoundly individual vision that is as much concerned with the photographer himself as it is with his subjects. Photography enabled Thesiger, as it has so many other photographers, to keep people and places where he wanted them: in a timeless state where the present slips into an imagined past which is itself outside time, enabling Thesiger himself to inhabit the timeless space of his imagination.

Finally it is, of course, time that makes this contemplation of Thesiger's photography possible. In many ways Thesiger was an accidental 'Photographer', not because his photography was marginal or incidental in any way, but because during the course of his life his photographic output shifted on its axis, from being a record of his journeys and his responses to the experiences he had and the people he encountered, to being something which has attracted attention in its own right. All histories are shaped by the patterns of their archiving and preservation and through the ways in which people engage with them, by what is done with them, how they are selected, and how they are published. These actions make them one thing and not another at given historical moments. It is how histories come to be written, and how Thesiger shifted from 'traveller and explorer' to 'traveller and photographer'. This volume is another moment in that history. Thesiger thus occupies a complex, ambiguous and sometimes problematic place in the history of visualization and cross-cultural relationships, but it is an undeniably rich one, shaped by equally complex responses to his work. And while the photographs remain informationally rich, they are also records of the ways in which Africa, and other parts of the world, have been imagined as a foil for the perceived degeneracy and destructiveness of 'civilization'. Aspects of time entangle the photographs in every facet of their existence, allowing Thesiger, and perhaps us, seduced by the beauty and romance of it all, to 'live once more in a vanished world'.[9]

Chapter 5

An Incidental Collection: Objects Donated by Wilfred Thesiger to the Pitt Rivers Museum

JEREMY COOTE

In September 1945 the then Curator of the Pitt Rivers Museum, T. K. Penniman, listed in the accessions register details of some eighty-five objects that had been donated by Wilfred Thesiger.[1] Unfortunately, no record survives concerning the circumstances of the donation. There is no trace of any correspondence between Thesiger and Penniman in the Museum's records, nor is there any evidence of the collection having been accompanied by any lists, notes or labels prepared by the donor. Most of the entries in the register are descriptive and provide no additional, contextual information, though the occasional entry does include information that must have come from the donor himself. For example, Penniman could not have known from an examination of the object itself that one of the Ethiopian cow-horn beakers had been 'sold as buffalo'. Despite the lack of documentary evidence, it seems likely that Thesiger delivered the collection to the Museum himself and explained it to Penniman. Indeed, one can easily imagine them working through the collection systematically as Penniman listed it in the register.[2]

It is not surprising that Thesiger should have given a collection to the Museum. He had read Modern History at Magdalen College from 1929 to 1933 and, according to his own account, visited the Museum frequently during this time, always finding it stimulating.[3] Indeed, he was later to express regret that he had not studied anthropology rather than history at Oxford.[4] More prosaically, that the donation was made in September 1945 may perhaps be understood in relation to the fact that two years previously Thesiger's mother had given up the large family home, The Milebrook in Radnorshire, to move to the flat in Tite Street in Chelsea that was to be Thesiger's London base until 1998. Thesiger was on leave in London from June to September 1945, and this would have been the first chance he had to help his mother sort out the crates of objects brought from The Milebrook.

In his war-affected 'double' annual report for the Museum for 1944–6, Penniman described Thesiger's donation of 1945 as an 'important and valuable gift'. Focussing on the Ethiopian material in the collection, Penniman described how the donated 'clothing and mule-trappings, of embroidered silk and velvet, weapons ordinary and ceremonial, and other material illustrating the life of a people not well represented in British collections, have enriched the Museum in a section which seemed most unlikely to develop', going on to remark how the donation had 'placed us greatly in the donor's debt'.[5]

The 1945 donation was not exclusively of Ethiopian material, however, nor indeed had all the material been collected by Thesiger himself. Rather it was a composite collection comprising material collected by his grandfather, his father and himself. The material from his grandfather consisted of three items he had brought back from South Africa after the Zulu War of 1879, in which – as General Lord Chelmsford – he had commanded the British troops. These were a 'witchdoctor's wand', a 'marriage ring', and a neck ornament said to have once been worn by Gaika, the youngest son of Chief Sandili of the ama-Ngquika Zulu. In his autobiography, Thesiger writes of watching history being made during his childhood in Ethiopia and links this to the assegais and other trophies brought back by his grandfather that adorned the walls of The Milebrook.[6] Such 'trophies' – like the adventure books he read – stirred Thesiger's imagination as he was growing up.

The material in the donation that had been collected by his father was mostly from Ethiopia, but also included objects from Turkish-controlled Armenia and the present-day Democratic Republic of Congo. The Armenian material comprised six pieces of Kurdish clothing

FIG.55 Ethiopian man's coat of black velvet, lined with red silk, decorated with silk embroidery and brass ornaments; 1,050 mm long. This coat is the one laid out on the table in Fig. 62.

collected in the Lake Van area. According to the accessions register these were collected in 1908, but it is more likely to have been in 1896–7 when Thesiger's father served as honorary Vice-Consul at Van at the time of the Armenian massacres. Thesiger writes of being fascinated by the watercolour sketches his father had painted of Kurds at this time 'in their distinctive and spectacular garb';[7] yet more evidence of the stirring of the young man's imagination and desire to travel and explore. The Congolese material comprises six examples of Kuba textiles and seven weapons, all of which his father had collected while serving as Consul in Boma, in what was then the Belgian Congo, in 1907–8.

The Ethiopian material consists of weapons and clothing, along with mule cloths and trappings. The weapons comprise seven shields (including two ceremonial examples and two used by boys), four swords and a spear. The clothing comprises both men's and women's garments that, according to the accessions register, had been given to Thesiger's parents 'as a compliment, according to Abyssinian custom'. They included a colourful headdress with a fringe of lion's hair and streamers in the Imperial Ethiopian colours of red, yellow and green, and an ornately embroidered man's coat of black velvet edged with yellow and lined with red silk and decorated with brass ornaments set with coloured stones (Fig. 55). The mule cloths and trappings are also impressive, demonstrating the accuracy of Thesiger's descriptions of the 'richly caparisoned'[8] and 'colourfully bedecked, trippling mules'[9] that he witnessed as a child in Addis Ababa.

Along with these objects collected by his grandfather and father, the 1945 donation included a number of pieces that had been collected by Thesiger himself. These include 'two heads of ecclesiastical standards' and an ecclesiastical jingle, along with five baskets and four horn beakers – all from Ethiopia. Among the most intriguing objects for anyone who has read Thesiger's *Danakil Diary* are those identified in the records as coming from that area of Ethiopia. These Thesiger must have acquired during his travels in 1930 and/or 1933–4. They include a deep, circular, coiled basket used for holding milk, two knives – a chief's knife and a commoner's one – and a goatskin waterbag (Fig. 56). According to the accessions register, the latter had been 'used by

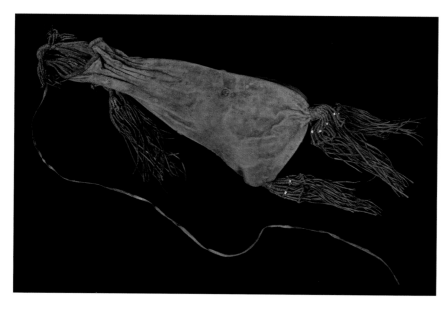

FIG.56 Danakil waterbag, made of goatskin tanned with bark and decorated with leather tassels and trade beads; 580 mm long. Perhaps the bag purchased by Thesiger on 12 March 1934 during his Awash expedition.

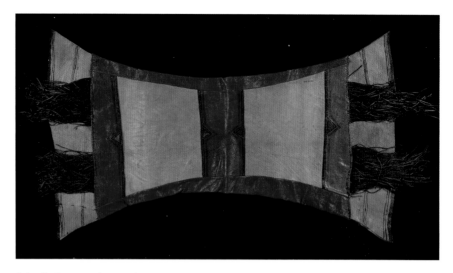

FIG. 57 Tuareg woman's saddle cushion, made of leather; 890 mm long. One of a number purchased by Thesiger from Tuareg refugees settled in Northern Darfur.

[the] donor throughout his travels in the Danakil country, 1933–34'. It is nice to think that this is the same waterskin that Thesiger records, in his diary entry for 12 March 1934, acquiring on the Kayeru Plain: 'bought a rather ornate waterskin from a Danakil. They chop up the bark from a mimosa tree and soak it in these skins for a day or two. Afterwards water carried in this skin is said to have a good taste and to be cool.'[10]

Along with these Ethiopian objects came two Somali knives that were presumably collected by Thesiger on the same journey. From his time as an Assistant District Commissioner in Northern Darfur, Sudan, came examples of leatherwork from the Tuareg who had settled in

FIG. 58 Interior of Wilfred Thesiger's house in Kutum, Northern Darfur, with weapons and trophies, some of which he later donated to the Pitt Rivers Museum, hanging on the wall (see Fig. 59). *Kutum, Sudan. 1935*.

Darfur after fleeing French Central Africa around 1910. In his auto-biography, Thesiger included a very brief account of these Tuareg, com-menting that 'they were skilled leatherworkers and I bought from them some decorated leather cushions which I still have',[11] presumably for-getting that he had given some to the Pitt Rivers in 1945 (Fig. 57). Also from Sudan came two throwing-knives, both bought in Darfur, though one probably originates from the Zande country in south-western Sudan. Thesiger wrote of decorating the walls of his house in Kutum 'with spears, swords, throwing-knives and the horns of animals I shot',[12] and it seems pretty clear that the throwing-knives in question are those he gave the Museum in 1945 (Figs. 58 and 59).

It was not until the occasion of the first exhibition of his photo-graphs at the Museum in 1993–4 – *Wilfred Thesiger's Photographs: A 'Most Cherished Possession'* – that Thesiger made another donation of objects. This comprised some of the things he had used during his crossings of the Rub' al Khali (Empty Quarter) in the 1940s, and included a goatskin bag in which he had carried his Leica camera, along with a camel-stick and a knife, sheath and belt. These were displayed for the duration of the exhibition, and subsequently donated to the Museum. A year later, after attending the opening of the Museum's exhibition of *Kuba Textiles*, which included a number of the pieces collected by his father that he had given in 1945, he made another small donation. This

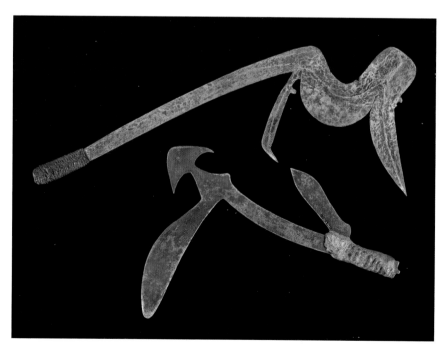

FIG.59 Two throwing-knives acquired by Thesiger while serving as Assistant District Commissioner in Northern Darfur and donated to the Pitt Rivers Museum in September 1945; 656 and 425 mm long. These throwing-knives hung on the wall of his house in Kutum (see Fig. 58).

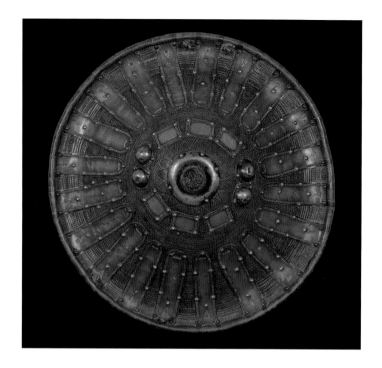

FIG.60 Ethiopian shield of embossed leather with strips of silver; 527 mm in diameter. Donated by Thesiger after the opening of the Pitt Rivers Museum's *Kuba Textiles* exhibition, which featured a number of textiles collected by his father.

comprised a framed Kuba raffia textile, along with an Ethiopian bishop's crown and an embossed Ethiopian shield (Fig. 60).[13]

Thesiger's final donation came to the Museum in 1998, via his friend and biographer Alexander Maitland. This is a mixed collection of forty objects, mostly from Ethiopia, but including three items from South Africa – presumably those presented to him by Chief Mangosuthu Buthelezi during his visit in 1997[14] – four more framed Kuba textiles, a blowpipe from Borneo that had been given to him at an eightieth birthday party at the Royal Geographical Society, and seven Arabian edged weapons. According to Maitland, Thesiger had kept the blades of these weapons cleaned and oiled and, with Maitland's help, had from time to time polished with great care the silver mountings and inlaid scabbards.[15] The Ethiopian material includes a number of rhinoceros-horn goblets and metal cups and bowls, along with three Afar edged weapons that he had presumably collected in the 1930s (Fig. 61). None of these bears the brass-decorated leather thong that would indicate that its owner had killed a man; but, intriguingly, hanging from the belt of the one to the left is a small leather pouch containing a glass bottle and a tiny horn spoon.

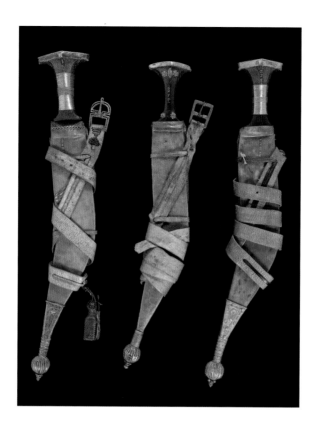

Even though the Pitt Rivers Museum is famed for the density of its displays, only part of its collections can ever be on exhibition to the public at one time. Of Thesiger's 1945 donation a few pieces have now been on permanent display for a number of years. Two of the Ethiopian mule cloths have been on display in the Museum's permanent textiles exhibition since 1982 and two of the Ethiopian hide shields, a double-edged sword and a Congolese spear-head have all been on display in the Museum's permanent exhibition of arms and armour in the upper gallery since 1994. A few other pieces have been selected for display in the Museum's series of special exhibitions from time to time. For example, three of the raffia cloths collected by Thesiger's father were included in the *Kuba Textiles* exhibition at the Museum in 1995, while an Ethiopian coiled basket was included in the Museum's *Objects Talk* exhibition in 2002–3.

The opportunity offered by the new exhibition focussed on Thesiger's African photographs to provide the Museum's public with a view of more of the objects he donated is very welcome. Until now few of the pieces have been exhibited or published, but perhaps the insights into the collection offered by the exhibition and this book will stimulate greater interest in the objects he gave. Many people, of course, will be primarily interested in those objects that seem to be of greatest personal relevance to the man himself and his travels: the Afar goatskin bag and knives come immediately to mind. Students of the art and material culture of Ethiopia, however, may want to pay more attention to the clothing and mule-trappings brought back from Addis Ababa by Thesiger's parents. As Penniman commented at the time, such material illustrates the life of a people 'not well represented in British collections' at a particular moment in time and would be well worth further scholarly attention.

In the context of the celebration of the centenary of Thesiger's birth, the final paragraphs of this essay must be devoted to exploring what we might learn about the man from the collections he gave the Museum. In doing so, one can perhaps consider what differences there might be between those things he gave away in 1945 and those he kept in his own collection at Tite Street until the 1990s. It would also be satisfying to be able to show how his collection illustrates his expressed aesthetic: 'my preference for drawings rather than paintings, my appreciation of line rather than colour'.[16] However, this remark seems to me to be better understood as a comment about his taste in art and photography than about his wider appreciation of the material world and the objects to be found in it. His books, for example, are full of evocative descriptions of the colours of landscapes and flowers, while one also senses from his writings an appreciation of craftsmanship, skill and truth to material.

Without more contemporary documentation it is difficult to say much for sure, but it does seem pretty clear that he had little sentimentality when it came to objects. For example, in 1945 he gave the Museum the goatskin bag that he had used on his travels in Afar country, a bag that had helped to keep him alive little more than a decade earlier. The fact that he donated so much material in 1945 also suggests that he did not want to be tied down by possessions. As his biographer Maitland records him saying in 1980, 'As such, possessions have meant very little to me.'[17] Even Thesiger, however, regretted the loss of one piece. As he recounts in his autobiography, after a visit to the trenches in Aden in 1918 his father had been presented with a magnificent dagger by a gathering of Arab sheikhs: 'I would have liked to wear it thirty years later when I travelled in the deserts of southern Arabia, but by then it had been lost.'[18] Even here, however, one wonders if it was the object itself or its association with his father, the sheikhs and the extraordinary experience for a seven-year-old boy of visiting the front line that made him regret the loss of this particular dagger. Clearly, however, some objects appealed to him for the quality of their workmanship and design. The Tuareg cushions would seem to fall into that category, as would his father's Kuba textiles, framed examples of which hung in the hall of the Tite Street flat until 1998. Indeed, it seems that textiles in particular appealed to him; in his autobiography he mentions every now and again purchasing examples for his mother and himself.

Maitland describes how the Tite Street flat 'was like a *catalogue raisonné* of his life and travels. Danakil *jilis* in tasselled sheaths hung beside framed black and white Kuba textiles from the Congo. There were silver-hilted Arab daggers and ancient swords in silver-inlaid scabbards.'[19] One is never aware, however, of Thesiger acting or sounding like a collector of artefacts. He did collect books, very methodically according to Maitland; and he collected natural history specimens – particularly birds, but also mammals, fossils and plants – for the Natural History Museum in London, as one means of funding his early travels.[20] At no point, however, does he seem to have collected objects in the same way. We might refer to the objects held at the Museum that were donated by him as 'the Thesiger collection', but they were not collected in any significant sense of the word; that is, there was nothing systematic about his acquisition of objects – it had no methodical, scientific purpose. Rather, objects were acquired as needed and as opportunities presented themselves, both as things to be used in his travels and as mementoes or souvenirs of the places where he travelled and the people with whom he lived. For the man himself, the 'sense of comradeship'[21] he found in travelling in remote, difficult and dangerous places with a few companions was the most important thing of all. The mapping, the collecting of natural history specimens, the photographs and writings for which he became so famous, even the exploration itself, were incidental.

The collections of objects at the Pitt Rivers Museum donated by Thesiger might also be seen as comprising a *catalogue raisonné* of his life (and the lives of his father and grandfather), but I am not sure he would have wanted us to see them like that – or at least not only like that. He would want us to admire the workmanship manifest in the objects, to catch the faint echoes they provide of peoples and places then little-touched by the modern world. We should appreciate them for their own qualities, not just for their association with him.

Part of the ambivalence of Thesiger's own attitude to objects is perhaps well caught by Ian Fairservice in his brief contrast between Thesiger's life in Maralal and his life in Chelsea in the late 1980s and early 1990s. Fairservice notes how in Maralal Thesiger's possessions were kept in a single trunk while the memories of his adventures were 'locked away in his mind'. In the months Thesiger spent each year in Chelsea, however, he was 'surrounded by his old books, photographs, and memorabilia'.[22] This dual existence perhaps satisfied two contrasting aspects of his personality: the need for a 'simple' life, without the burden of possessions and the demands of urban civilization, and the need for a 'complex' life in which his place in British society was renewed and reinvigorated.

Today, the objects Thesiger donated to the Museum may be valued primarily for their association with the celebrated traveller and photographer. They may also be valued, however, for the information they embody about the people who made and used them and the historic moments of their creation and use. As yet, few of the objects Thesiger gave the Museum have been subjected to detailed research. Indeed, in many ways, the collection remains relatively undocumented in contrast to the extremely well-documented life of Thesiger himself. Certainly the objects he gave the Museum have received far less attention than his photographs. Taken together, the combined legacy of his writings, photographs and objects amounts to an important set of documents about the material and visual history of the places in which he lived and travelled, particularly Ethiopia. Without doubt they have enriched the Museum and, as Penniman noted sixty-five years ago, 'placed us greatly in the donor's debt'.

ACKNOWLEDGEMENTS

For their comments on an early draft of this essay, I am grateful to Alexander Maitland, Christopher Morton and Chris Sharpe.

Chapter 6

Wilfred Thesiger's Photograph Collection at the Pitt Rivers Museum

CHRISTOPHER MORTON
AND SCHUYLER JONES

*Schuyler Jones, Director of the Pitt Rivers Museum
from 1985 to 1996, writes:*

I first met Wilfred Thesiger in Edinburgh in 1962 when he was awarded the Livingstone Medal by the Scottish Geographical Society for his explorations in Arabia. Then for some years our paths did not cross. An occasional letter was exchanged and one or two telephone calls. Often he was away when I tried to arrange a meeting by telephone and I then had entertaining conversations with Mollie Emtage, his housekeeper. In any case, during much of that period I was in Afghanistan and he was living and travelling in East Africa, and earlier, when I was living and travelling in East Africa, he was in Arabia, so it was not until later when I was in Oxford and Wilfred was spending, uncharacteristically, more time at his flat in Chelsea that we began to see each other at intervals.

That Wilfred had settled in later life in Maralal in northern Kenya was always a joke between us, because Maralal seemed to be the only place in the world I had reached before him, arriving some eight years ahead on this occasion. While based in Maralal he made a series of journeys with Frank Steele – the only European who ever accompanied him for any length of time on his travels. Later, comparing notes, we discovered that I had also preceded him in the Bashgal and Waigal Valleys of eastern Afghanistan. 'Oh well,' said Wilfred with mock resignation,

'I'll give you those. After all I still have the Empty Quarter.' After a pause he added, with a twinkle in his eye, 'And a *few* other places.'

For years Wilfred had regularly spent a couple of the spring months in his Chelsea home, a spacious top floor flat with a view of the Thames from the sitting room window. We passed many hours together there looking at his photographs, going through his wonderful library, which included such rarities as a copy of the subscribers' 1926 edition of T. E. Lawrence's *Seven Pillars of Wisdom*, and talking about remote regions of Africa and Asia which we knew from our travels. Sometimes we sat in the kitchen, Wilfred making coffee with a pinch of cardamom in it to remind us of the Middle East. Sometimes we walked down to a nearby restaurant, he in later years taking my arm for support. I would often take him to various appointments around London as I had the car, Wilfred explaining that he only drove in East Africa where there was plenty of room and miles of roads without another vehicle in sight.

When we were together in Oxford we sometimes went to the library at Magdalen College to spend an hour or two examining Lawrence's original maps from his travels in Arabia. Wilfred was a great admirer of Lawrence, often remarking how much he regretted never having met him. Born in 1888, Lawrence was only twenty-two years older than Wilfred and, of course, Lawrence had been at Oxford, but their paths never crossed. Another man whom Wilfred admired greatly was Charles Doughty, author of the justly famed *Travels in Arabia Deserta* (1888). The travels and writings of these two explorers may have influenced Wilfred's career nearly as much as had his boyhood experiences in Abyssinia.

In between events at Oxford, Wilfred was occasionally in my office at the Pitt Rivers Museum or out in the Museum looking at artefacts that he had donated many years before. Among other things, we discussed the long-term deposit of his remarkable collection of photographs. Wilfred modestly claimed that he really knew nothing about photography, had never taken a colour picture and certainly never intended to, and had no training whatever in photography. But his photographs from Arabia, the marshes of southern Iraq, Kurdistan, Iran and Afghanistan are some of the finest I have ever seen. One only has to look through *Desert, Marsh and Mountain* (1979) to see that he was a master of the photographic image with an unerring eye for composition.

At some point I had written to him to suggest that his photographic negatives and prints might find a permanent home in the archives of the Pitt Rivers Museum in Oxford. Usually a prompt and considerate correspondent, he did not reply at once. But then, out of the blue many months later, I suddenly had a letter from him, dated 16 May 1991. In this he refers to my earlier letter and goes on to say that he would like to discuss the possibility of depositing his Arabian and African photographs in the Pitt Rivers Museum.

This led to some informal discussions in Oxford and London regarding the proposed gift. Although Wilfred had at one time considered donating his photographs to the Royal Geographical Society, these plans soon fell by the wayside. Apparently what had convinced him that the Pitt Rivers Museum was the best repository for his collection was the speed with which we were able to produce artefacts he had donated to the Museum years before and the fine condition in which he found them (Fig. 62). He also saw that we had a remarkable archive of unique early photographs from different parts of the world, all catalogued in an efficient data-retrieval system.

FIG. 62 Wilfred Thesiger with Schuyler Jones (centre) and his friend William Delafield (right) examining two objects collected by his father, an embroidered Ethiopian coat (see Fig. 55) and a lion's mane headdress, both donated to the Pitt Rivers Museum in 1945. *Oxford, UK. Photograph by Malcolm Osman. June 1991.*

Wilfred was essentially a nineteenth-century man. He often expressed the view that the most destructive invention ever made by man was the internal combustion engine. While agreeing with him on this, I always added Mikhail Kalashnikov's AK-47 of which no less than seventy-three million have been made and distributed worldwide.

———— • ◆ • ————

Christopher Morton, Curator of Photographs at the Pitt Rivers Museum, writes:

Wilfred Thesiger in Africa is the third major exhibition of Thesiger's photographs organized by the Pitt Rivers Museum since 1993, an unprecedented series for the Museum but one that reflects both the historical significance and enduring popularity of the collection. As the following brief history demonstrates, these exhibitions have often travelled far from Oxford, and brought the collection to a wider audience in the UK, Africa, the Middle East and America.

Plans for an exhibition of Wilfred Thesiger's photographs began at the time that he offered the collection to the Museum in 1991. During one of his occasional visits to the Museum, partly to see his father's collections that he had presented nearly half a century earlier, Schuyler Jones remarked that it would be a fine thing to have an exhibition of his photographs in the Museum. 'What a good idea!' he answered, 'There has never been an exhibition of my photographs in this country.' And so in February 1992 Jones wrote to him with a draft exhibition proposal, drawn up by the then curator of photographs, Elizabeth Edwards. This proposal suggested a wide-ranging retrospective of his travel photography:

> . . . the exhibition will function as something of a 'retrospective', a fitting approach from us as the museum entrusted with the long-term care of the collection for the historical record. The central theme should be 'the journey' and the exhibition should aim to encapsulate Mr. Thesiger's travels. The idea of 'the journey' will operate at three levels: 1. The first is quite straightforward in that travelling [and] journeying are intrinsic to the photographs themselves; 2. A chronological arrangement will suggest a 'biographical

journey', Mr. Thesiger's life as a traveller, explorer and photographer; 3. The museum visitor will be given a sense of 'journey' in the physical arrangement of the exhibition, establishing a travel narrative. Working their way through the exhibition, the visitor, in a sense, 'follows in Mr. Thesiger's footsteps' or 'accompanies him on his travels' through the photographs.

Within this framework I would suggest that the subject emphasis should tend towards the ethnographic (in broad terms), reflecting the Museum's specific interests and indeed what the visitor expects from us. The 'ethnographic' material could then be positioned, both environmentally and visually, through landscape photographs.

The space should be organised into 7 or 8 discrete areas (modules) linked by narrower 'passages'. There should be one module for each major area of travel (say Marsh Arabs, Empty Quarter, Abyssinia, Kurdistan, Afghanistan, India, Kenya). These modules would be linked by travel sequences in the passage areas, series of photographs arranged like contact sheets (in preference one would use enlargements of actual contact sheets where possible e.g. arriving at Marsh Arab settlement across the water) which would introduce the visitor to the next section at the same time as suggesting 'journeying' and the passage of time.

The exhibition should comprise 70–80 photographs, using 12" x 16" prints, or occasionally larger 20" x 16", with linking series.[1]

The following month the Museum received a letter from Frank Steele, Thesiger's friend and former travelling companion in Kenya, who wrote:

I have just returned from a fortnight spent in N. Kenya with my old friend Wilfred Thesiger. Unfortunately his eyesight is deteriorating and he can read and write only with difficulty . . . He is of course immensely pleased with [the] idea of the exhibition and likes the general outline drawn up by Elizabeth Edwards.[2]

In early 1993, as preparations for the exhibition were in full swing, and as deadlines loomed, the Museum urgently needed a written foreword for the exhibition publication. Given that Thesiger was still then living in Maralal for most of each year, this was not a straightforward

FIG.63 Pages from one of Wilfred Thesiger's photograph albums, which he described in *Visions of a Nomad* as his 'most cherished possession'. These two pages show photographs taken during the coronation ceremonies of Emperor Haile Selassie.

exercise. In a letter to Thesiger in January, Elizabeth Edwards wrote that 'we have decided to call the exhibition "Wilfred Thesiger's Photographs – a Most Cherished Possession", using your own description of your collection. I hope you like it', and asked whether he might draft the text of the foreword with the photographer Adrian Arbib, who was to visit the area later that month. An edited version of the foreword text was subsequently sent back to Thesiger via Frank Steele, in February. The final version was returned to the Museum at the end of March, with a number of revisions to some of the revealing remarks originally made to Arbib. The original text, for instance, included the insight that:

> On one occasion in 1961 some Maasai genuinely refused to be photographed. I was anxious to do so. I went off a little distance, walked about and stared through my camera at various objects.

They followed me. One asked if he could look through the camera
and I let him do so. He pointed it at a friend. After that the ice was
broken. The laughing crowd looked at each other through it and
I took the photographs I wanted.[3]

Although Steele remarked that this anecdote had been omitted since
it was 'totally out of keeping with the rest',[4] it shortly afterwards appeared
in print in Thesiger's book *My Kenya Days* (1994), dictated to Alexander
Maitland at around the same time, where Thesiger describes it as happening on a journey with John Newbould.[5] In the final version of the
foreword, Thesiger also added that in the Pitt Rivers Museum he had
found a suitable home for his 'most cherished possession', by which he
principally referred to his extraordinary collection of seventy-one albums
of photographs (Fig. 63): 'During the four years, 1929 to 1933, I was at
Oxford, I frequently visited the Pitt Rivers Museum. I always found it

FIG.64 Wilfred Thesiger at the opening of the Pitt Rivers Museum's touring exhibition of his work, *Wilfred Thesiger's Photographs: A 'Most Cherished Possession'*. Oxford, UK. Photograph by Rob Judges. June 1993.

stimulating, and what I learnt there helpful in later years. When I saw the Photographic Department on a recent visit to Oxford, I realized at once that this was the place for my photographs.'[6] This was a sentiment that he was to echo in the acknowledgements to *My Kenya Days* (1994), written at the same time, in which he recalls being impressed by the 'care they took to preserve and treat scientifically the photographs and negatives they had acquired . . . I have now presented my complete collection of photographs, prints and negatives to the Pitt Rivers Museum in recognition of the four happy years I spent at Oxford.'[7]

The exhibition *Wilfred Thesiger's Photographs: A 'Most Cherished Possession'*, which was opened by Princess Sarvath of Jordan and Wilfred Thesiger at an event on 16 June 1993 (Fig. 64), ran until 27 February 1994, and was seen by over 64,000 people (Fig. 65).

Mindful of potential criticism that the Museum's presentation of Thesiger's romantic images of what were by then very troubled regions – it was after all the period of Saddam Hussein's persecution of the Marsh Arabs and Kurds – might be politically naïve, distorted or complicit, a panel was erected within the exhibition space showing newspaper coverage – both positive and negative – from all of the regions covered in the exhibition.

Soon after the exhibition closed in Oxford, the seventy-nine framed prints embarked on an unprecedented tour, for the Pitt Rivers Museum at least, of Africa and the Middle East, organized by the Visual Arts Department of the British Council. In April 1994 the exhibition opened (with Thesiger present) at the British Council in Nairobi, Kenya, where nearly 200 people attended the opening event. In May it travelled to the National Museum of Ethiopia in Addis Ababa, where initial problems meant that it opened later than planned, but was well attended by over 3,000 people in just six days. In June the exhibition was at the British Council in Khartoum, Sudan, and in July at the InterContinental Hotel in Dubai, United Arab Emirates. On 21 August the exhibition opened at the Bahrain National Museum, where it ran until 13 September, before moving on to Oman and the Al Bustan Palace Hotel in Muscat until the end of October. The British Council had also hoped

FIG.65 *Wilfred Thesiger's Photographs: A 'Most Cherished Possession'* on display at the Pitt Rivers Museum. *Oxford, UK. Photograph by Malcolm Osman. 1993.*

to show the exhibition at the British Council in Riyadh, Saudi Arabia, but funding restrictions meant that this did not happen. In January 1996, Sean Williams of the British Council finally confirmed that the exhibition was not to travel to Syria as planned: 'Our office in Syria was keen to have the Thesiger exhibition . . . to tour to its three main centres in the country. Regrettably, they have now already agreed to host another exhibition . . . and could not afford to take on another arts tour.'[8]

A Most Cherished Possession arrived back at the British Council workshops in April 1995, where the prints and frames were checked over in preparation for a further tour, this time to the USA, organized by the Southeast Museum of Photography in Daytona, Florida, where it showed from 11 July to 25 August, before opening on 18 September at the University Art Gallery, University of Massachusetts Dartmouth, where it ran until 21 October. Against hopes, take-up for the exhibition in the USA proved disappointing. Partly this was for historical reasons, with the USA even then having relatively less interest in the Arab world than the UK did, but also partly because of the fact that Thesiger's social background, world-view, and consequently his photography, had less appeal to American curators and their audiences, increasingly interested as they were in the modernist and post-modernist aesthetics that dominated the US galleries.[9]

With the exhibition on its way back to the UK in December 1995, the possibility of further UK venues emerged. When the British Council's hopes of returning the exhibition to Saudi Arabia and Syria during 1996 failed to materialize, an agreement was made with the Russell-Cotes Art Gallery and Museum in Bournemouth to host the exhibition, which took place from late 1996 until February 1997. In April of that year the exhibition (excluding the African photographs) travelled to the Oriental Museum, University of Durham, where it was exhibited until July.

The success of the British Council tour of *A Most Cherished Possession* in Africa led to the suggestion that a further selection of Thesiger's Ethiopian photographs be produced to celebrate the centenary of the founding of the British Embassy in Addis Ababa, in June 1996. Since Thesiger's father had acted as Consul-General there between 1909 and 1919, and given that Thesiger had been born there in 1910, this idea seemed particularly appropriate. Thesiger himself was delighted at the prospect of this exhibition, to be held at the Embassy, and asked whether it might include some of the images of Emperor Menelik from his family albums, as well as photographs of the Legation compound as it had been.[10] Although the British Council favoured including such historical material in the exhibition, it was felt that since the prints were possibly to be donated to the National Museum of Ethiopia after the exhibition closed, a 'straight photo exhibition' would be preferable, without the historical dimension. In November 1995, the curator of the exhibition, Elizabeth Edwards, noted that she had 'selected only from the 1959–60 photographs. The earlier material of the coronation [of Haile Selassie] and the court etc., although historically fascinating, might be seen as politically fraught in one direction or another.'[11] At this stage, the idea of donating the material to the National Museum of Ethiopia was also abandoned in favour of a permanent display in the British Embassy, a decision favoured by the Museum. Keen as ever to cast an eye over how his photographs were being treated, Thesiger looked over the prints before they were sent out to Ethiopia for the 1996 centenary celebrations, during one of his occasional visits to the Museum, and was said to be 'very pleased' with them.[12]

In 2003 a series of discussions between the Museum's curator of photographs Elizabeth Edwards and the then curator of the National Trust's Fox Talbot Museum,[13] Michael Gray, led to a proposal for an exhibition of Thesiger's travel photographs of Iraq. In March 2003 a coalition force led by the USA had embarked on a military invasion of Iraq, which lasted for six weeks. In the turmoil that ensued there was widespread dismay that the rich cultural heritage of the country might have suffered irrevocable harm, heightened by the looting, in mid-April, of the National Museum of Iraq in Baghdad, and the inability of coalition forces to protect it. During the invasion, the full extent of Saddam Hussein's repression of the Madan (Marsh Arabs) during and after the First Iraq War in 1991 was also brought to wider public awareness, as the environmental and cultural impact of the draining of the marshes gained wider acknowledgement. While arts and cultural institutions in the UK did not seek to enter the political domain, there was a sense that highlighting Iraqi arts and culture at such a time was an appropriate response to mainstream media stereotypes of the country. For instance, in September 2003 an exhibition of Baghdad-based artist Kerim Rissin's work opened at the Deluxe Gallery in Hoxton Square, London, called *Before.After.Now*. In its invitation to the private view, the Gallery claimed it to be 'the first exhibition of its kind since the war. It's an attempt to give a space for the Iraqi voice to be heard, and a forum for Londoners to explore a culture . . . of which they have had very little first-hand experience.' Another important context for the Thesiger exhibition, of course, was the death of Wilfred Thesiger himself on 24 August 2003, shortly before a major project was to begin at the Museum to catalogue his collection, funded by Sheikh Zayed bin Sultan Al Nahyan. Thesiger's death meant that his photographs were formally acquired by the Museum via the UK government's Acceptance in Lieu (of inheritance tax) scheme in 2004.[14]

The collaborative exhibition between the Museum and the National Trust at the Fox Talbot Museum, *Wilfred Thesiger's Iraq 1949–1958: Photographs of Travel*, opened on 29 July 2004 and was on display in Lacock until 31 October of that year. Writing to the Museum in early August, the National Trust praised the Museum curatorial team,[15] commenting that 'the exhibition itself at Lacock looks absolutely great and first reaction by the public is extremely positive. The phone has been ringing off the hook with enquiries about the show following the extensive press coverage. I think the show is going to be a roaring success.'[16] Although not originally envisaged, the opportunity arose for the exhibition to return to Oxford in December 2004, as the Museum's exhibition *Seeing Lhasa* was about to close and a stop-gap display was required until May 2005 before the next scheduled special exhibition, *Treasured Textiles*. Due to delays in producing the textile exhibition, *Wilfred Thesiger's Iraq* (Fig. 66) remained on display for an additional full year, closing in April 2006, having been seen by approximately 200,000 people.

A number of other significant international exhibitions have included Thesiger's photography. In June 2000 the Fondation Cartier pour l'Art Contemporain, Paris, mounted the major exhibition *Le désert*, which explored historic and contemporary representations of desert landscapes. This featured a number of Thesiger's Rub' al Khali (Empty Quarter) photographs, known to a French audience through *Le désert des déserts* (1978), the French translation of *Arabian Sands*

(1959). This exhibition subsequently travelled to the Centro Cultural de la Fundación 'la Caixa', Barcelona, and the Centro Andaluz de Arte Contemporáneo, Seville, in 2001, under the Spanish exhibition title *El Desierto*. Another exhibition of interest took place at Eton College Library in 2004, where Thesiger had donated his archive of notebooks, family correspondence and drafts of his books, in memory of his school days spent there.

A number of exhibitions, mostly of Thesiger's Arabian photographs, have been successfully held in the United Arab Emirates, many of them organized or facilitated by the publisher Ian Fairservice, who has produced a number of Thesiger's books (such as *Crossing the Sands* (1999)). These have included exhibitions at Motivate's Arabian Gallery in Dubai, and notably an exhibition at the Cultural Foundation of Abu Dhabi in 2004. Wilfred Thesiger is particularly highly regarded in the emirates of Dubai and Abu Dhabi, not just for his travels, writings and photographs of the Rub' al Khali (Empty Quarter), but also due to his enduring friendship with the first president of the United Arab Emirates, Sheikh Zayed bin Sultan Al Nahyan (1918–2004). In the UAE, Thesiger is still affectionately known as 'Mubarak bin London' – the name he was

FIG.66 *Wilfred Thesiger's Iraq 1949– 1958: Photographs of Travel* on display at the Pitt Rivers Museum. This exhibition was previously shown at the National Trust's Fox Talbot Museum in Lacock. *Oxford, UK. Photograph by Suzy Prior. 2005.*

given at the time of his Empty Quarter crossings in the 1940s. This relationship was celebrated in 2008 by a collaborative venture between the Pitt Rivers Museum and the Abu Dhabi Authority for Culture and Heritage to develop a permanent exhibition of Thesiger's photography at the newly renovated Jahili Fort in Al Ain (Fig. 67). This display is now a major visitor attraction, and celebrates Thesiger's relationship to the region and its people, as well as his popularity as a photographer and travel writer.

In 1999 Sheikh Zayed indicated that he wished to fund a project to digitally copy and catalogue Thesiger's photographs, and so in 2000, as the first part of the project, the negatives were sent in batches, beginning with those of Africa, to the stills department of Pinewood Studios to be scanned on to Kodak Photo CD. Although originally envisaged to take five months, the digitization of the collection eventually took almost a year, and was still not entirely completed, partly because of an underestimation of the size of the collection, but also because Thesiger's early photography was not taken on roll film, and hence could not be processed in an automated manner.

Although the second phase of the project, a detailed catalogue of all 38,000 images in the collection, seemed to be imminent in mid-2000,

FIG.67 The gallery in Jahili Fort at Al Ain, recently restored with a permanent display of Wilfred Thesiger's photographs. *Al Ain, United Arab Emirates. Photograph by Torsten Seidel. 2008.*

and with the necessary funds seemingly secured from Sheikh Zayed to carry out the work, the cataloguing project did not get under way until three years later, in October 2003. Three full-time staff members worked on the project for a year, and as a result produced a full catalogue of all 38,000 negatives in the collection, cross-referenced to those prints included in Thesiger's own albums.

As already mentioned, *Wilfred Thesiger in Africa* is the third major exhibition of Thesiger's photography to be organized by the Museum since 1993, a fact that reflects both the enduring appeal of one of the most significant of twentieth-century British travel writers and photographers, but also that in donating his photographs to the Museum, Thesiger has 'placed us greatly in the donor's debt,' as curator T. K. Penniman noted in another context in the 1940s. The exhibition owes its inception to the vision of William Delafield, a long-term supporter of the Museum, whose charitable trust offered its backing should the Museum wish to mount a centenary exhibition. In early 2007 the Museum presented a proposal for a centenary exhibition to the Trust, stating that:

> 2010 sees the centenary of Wilfred Thesiger's birth at the Legation compound in Addis Ababa. The experience of these early years in Ethiopia was something that remained of real importance to Thesiger throughout his life, and something that he felt was formative . . . a focus on his African travels and photography will enable the story of his life to be placed in the context of his early experiences, and come full circle to his decision to settle in later life in Kenya. The influence of Africa spans the entirety of Thesiger's life . . . [17]

From the Museum's perspective, a focus on Africa also has the benefit of introducing a lesser known area of his photography, in comparison to his Arabian and Marsh Arab photographs. Given that the Museum's most recent exhibition of Thesiger's photographs had focussed upon his images of Iraq, a focus on his African photography would allow audiences to discover much material that had not been exhibited or published previously, as well as a chance to follow some of his less familiar travels on the continent. In addition, the fact that the exhibition is being held in the new special exhibition gallery in the recently completed extension to the Museum means that we have been able to include a small selection of Ethiopian objects collected by the Thesiger family and donated to the Museum over many years.

An African focus also afforded the opportunity to examine Thesiger's development as a photographer, from his first exploration of the Awash River among the Afar (Danakil) of Ethiopia in 1933–4, to his photographs of Kenya in the 1960s, 1970s and 1980s, a period spanning half a century. The attempt to see points of change and continuity in his photography has not been attempted in this manner previously, and was something that an exhibition of his African photographs could at last consider. Elizabeth Edwards's exploration in this volume of the notion of time, and timelessness, in Thesiger's photography gives us an important new perspective on his work.

While being predominantly a record of travel, Thesiger's photographs are a curious one in that regard, often lacking the sort of documentation or other specific detail that such an archive might be expected to include. It is a spontaneous rather than systematic record, a summation of his many aesthetic encounters along the way. It is painterly by nature; we see grand landscapes given scale and romantic grandeur by a carefully positioned individual, and portraits that hark back to Renaissance paintings. It is a sensual record also, taking delight in the tones and textures of skin, textile, landscape and architecture. The subjects and places that populate Thesiger's photographs are not fleetingly glimpsed, but rather fully engaged with, and given full attention.

This was a personal record after all, with little thought for posterity or publication, at least initially. Thesiger was deeply interested in the peoples of Africa whom he travelled with and among, and yet he had little time for academic anthropological writing about those cultures, judging it 'almost unreadable'.[18] Yet his perspective as a longer-term resident, such as among the Marsh Arabs and in Kenya, did lead to valuable anthropological insights, and did produce a valuable visual record of anthropological interest. An example of this is the (unpublished) ethnographic study that Thesiger made of Samburu circumcision practices. Although the anthropologist Paul Spencer, Thesiger acknowledged, had written two detailed books describing Samburu society and culture, the books had only cursorily mentioned initiation, since Spencer had left Kenya before witnessing one of these infrequent ceremonies. 'I was astonished that he dismissed circumcision in a few paragraphs,' wrote Thesiger, since

the attendant ceremonies are the most important in the lives of the Samburu . . . the very structure of the tribe is based on their system of age grades . . . I was present when new age-sets were introduced in 1960, in 1976 and in 1990; on the last two occasions I was involved to some extent in the proceedings, owing to my close relationship with the families of certain initiates; as a result I began to understand the importance to them of these rituals and ceremonies.[19]

This then was Thesiger's perspective, and ultimately his contribution – an attuned sensitivity towards, and affinity with, the subjective experiences of individuals, rather than with the abstractions of anthropology. His was an intensely personal relationship with Africa, and yet his photographs accommodate us within them as viewers; not just Thesiger's Africa, but a vision for all to share.

Chapter 7

Wilfred Thesiger's Photographs of Africa: A Centenary Selection

PHILIP N. GROVER
AND CHRISTOPHER MORTON

'I am certain that the first nine years of my life have influenced every-thing that followed,' wrote Wilfred Thesiger in 1994, the opening line of his memoir *My Kenya Days*.[1] As he saw it, Africa set his life on its course and it is therefore fitting that it should provide the focus for this cen-tenary volume. An engagement with Africa spanned nearly the entire length of Thesiger's life, from his birth in 1910 and early years in Addis Ababa, his first journeys of exploration in the early 1930s, administra-tive postings in the Sudan and subsequent wartime experiences, to his eventual return to Ethiopia in 1959 and his travels and residence in Kenya until the last years of his life. The photographs which follow – and, indeed, those which appear throughout the book – have been selected as representative of many of the themes in his work, but they are undoubtedly also some of his finest and most striking images. Drawn from over 17,000 negatives, or rather more than two-fifths of his entire photographic output, they span the greater part of his life and show people and places in Ethiopia[2], Chad, Sudan, Morocco, Tanzania[3] and Kenya; the last picture in our selection was taken near his home in Maralal in Kenya in 1983.

Thesiger's very first published photographs were taken in Africa, appearing with a series of articles about his 1933–4 Awash expedition, and his photographs accompanied his writings throughout his life.[4]

In fact, Thesiger considered his photography integral to his writing, not just as a key to memory but as a valuable addition to the published record.[5] It is also true, however, that from the beginning the photographs were secondary to the writing – an accompaniment rather than the main course – but an elevation of image took place from the time of his *Desert, Marsh and Mountain* (1979), and reached its fullest expression with the publication of *Visions of a Nomad* (1987).[6] Exhibitions followed, and in 2001 his final authored book of photographs appeared, *A Vanished World.*[7] What is perhaps surprising about these various publications, however, is that relatively few images of Africa were included, the emphasis being on his celebrated travels in Arabia and elsewhere.[8] This centenary volume attempts to redress the balance somewhat, with the fullest publication to date of the diverse range of his photographs of Africa, as well as early photographs from his family albums, including over a hundred previously unpublished images.

ABYSSINIA

Fig.68 OPPOSITE TOP Abyssinian warriors in front of Emperor
Menelik's palace. *Addis Ababa, Ethiopia. Photograph by Wilfred Gilbert
Thesiger. Circa 1909.*

Fig.69 OPPOSITE BOTTOM Wilfred Thesiger's father being escorted
into Addis Ababa to present his credentials to Lij Yasu, heir apparent
to Emperor Menelik. *Addis Ababa, Ethiopia. Photographer unknown.
December 1909.*

Fig.70 ABOVE Procession through the streets of Addis Ababa
during the coronation of the Empress Zauditu. *Addis Ababa, Ethiopia.
Photographer unknown. February 1917.*

FIG.71 ABOVE An Abyssinian warrior, carrying a rifle and shield and wearing a lion's mane headdress, at the coronation ceremonies of Emperor Haile Selassie. *Addis Ababa, Ethiopia. November 1930.*

FIG.72 OPPOSITE TOP Procession through Addis Ababa during the coronation ceremonies of Emperor Haile Selassie. *Addis Ababa, Ethiopia. Photographer unknown. November 1930.*

FIG.73 OPPOSITE BOTTOM People gathered at the Feast of Epiphany for the blessing of the waters by priests in Addis Ababa. *Addis Ababa, Ethiopia. 1933.*

FIG.74 OPPOSITE TOP Wilfred Thesiger's expedition party crossing the Webi Shebeli. *Arussi, Ethiopia. October 1933.*

FIG.75 OPPOSITE BOTTOM The swamps of southern Aussa. *Aussa, Ethiopia. April 1934.*

FIG.76 BELOW Sinter formations in the south-east corner of Lake Abhebad. *Lake Abhebad, Ethiopia. April 1934.*

FIG.77 OPPOSITE TOP Abyssinian 'Patriots', as the resistance forces were known, armed with captured Italian rifles. 'Some of the Patriots vowed never to cut their hair until they had driven the Italians out,' Thesiger noted. *Gojjam, Ethiopia. 1941.*

FIG.78 OPPOSITE BOTTOM Patriot soldier photographed during Wingate's rounding-up of the Italian forces driven out of Gojjam. *Agibar, Ethiopia. June 1941.*

FIG.79 ABOVE Patriot soldier photographed during Wingate's rounding-up of the Italian forces driven out of Gojjam. *Agibar, Ethiopia. June 1941.*

CHAD

FIG.80 ABOVE Wilfred Thesiger's expedition party at Bardai in the Tibesti Mountains. *Bardai, Chad. 1938.*

FIG.81 OPPOSITE TOP Tebu man in the Tibesti Mountains. *Bardai, Chad. 1938.*

FIG.82 OPPOSITE BOTTOM Landscape around Emi Koussi (11,204 feet), the highest mountain in Tibesti. *Tibesti, Chad. 1938.*

FIG.83 OVERLEAF The Nanamsena gorge, near Aouzou, in the Tibesti Mountains. Thesiger noted that a 'water-course wound between sheer cliffs that were from four to seven hundred feet high, though sometimes only twenty-five feet apart, and never more than ninety'. *Tibesti, Chad. 1938.*

SUDAN

FIG.84 ABOVE Thesiger's Nuer porters trekking through waterlogged terrain in Western Nuerland. *Western Upper Nile, Sudan. 1938.*

FIG.85 OPPOSITE TOP Nuer men swimming their cattle across the Nile below Lake No. *Western Upper Nile, Sudan. 1938.*

FIG.86 OPPOSITE BOTTOM Nuer men hunting hippo, a meat prized for its high fat content. After harpooning the animal, 'the carcass was towed ashore and cut up, and the meat carried off to the various camps'. *Western Upper Nile, Sudan. 1938.*

FIG.87 BELOW Nuer men in the papyrus swamp during a hippo hunt. *Western Upper Nile, Sudan. 1938.*

FIG.88 OPPOSITE TOP Shilluk man with coiffure and feather decoration. *Upper Nile, Sudan. 1939.*

FIG.89 OPPOSITE BOTTOM Portrait of a Shilluk youth wearing head and neck ornaments. *Upper Nile, Sudan. 1939.*

FIG.90 OPPOSITE Portrait of a Shilluk man. *Upper Nile, Sudan. 1939.*

FIG.91 ABOVE A Shilluk man carrying a wooden club. *Upper Nile, Sudan. 1939.*

FIG.92 OVERLEAF Dinka men with spears and ambatch parrying shields at a funeral dance near Malakal. *Upper Nile, Sudan. 1939.*

FIG.93 OPPOSITE TOP Dinka men at a funeral dance near Malakal.
Upper Nile, Sudan. 1939.

FIG.94 OPPOSITE BOTTOM Dinka men and women at a funeral
dance near Malakal. *Upper Nile, Sudan. 1939.*

FIG.95 ABOVE Drummer at a Dinka funeral dance near Malakal.
Upper Nile, Sudan. 1939.

MOROCCO

FIG.96 ABOVE The famous Bab Mansour gate in the city wall at
Meknes. This photograph was probably not taken by Thesiger, but
the print from which it is reproduced was presumably purchased by
him during his first visit to Morocco in 1937. *Meknes, Morocco.*
Photographer unknown. Circa 1937.

FIG.97 OPPOSITE Street scene in the former imperial capital of Fez.
This photograph was probably acquired by Thesiger during his first
visit to Morocco. *Fez, Morocco. Photographer unknown. Circa 1937.*

FIG.98 OPPOSITE Houses and their inhabitants at Imdras in the
High Atlas Mountains. *Imdras, Morocco. 1955.*

FIG.99 ABOVE Buildings at a settlement near Telouet in the High
Atlas Mountains. *Imerhrane, Morocco. 1955.*

FIG.100 OPPOSITE Children. The boy in the background may be imitating the photographer. *Imdras, Morocco. 1955.*

FIG.101 ABOVE Profile study of a girl showing her cropped hairstyle. *Amesker, Morocco. 1955.*

FIG.102 ABOVE Kasbahs at Ghasat in the High Atlas Mountains, with Irhil M'Goun (13,356 feet) rising in the distance. *Ghasat, Morocco. August 1955.*

FIG.103 OPPOSITE TOP Children at a settlement in the High Atlas Mountains. *Ait Ayoub, Morocco. 1955.*

FIG.104 OPPOSITE BOTTOM Kasbah, or fortress with surrounding quarter, at Amejgag in the High Atlas Mountains. Many kasbahs were built in the late seventeenth century by the ruler Moulay Ismail during his military campaigns to unify the country. *Amejgag, Morocco. 1955.*

FIG.105 OVERLEAF Houses built on to the rock face at Ait Hamed, where Thesiger lodged with Khalifa Haji Umr: 'He received us friendlily and gave us a good room.' *Ait Hamed, Morocco. August 1955.*

FIG.106 OPPOSITE TOP The *souk* (market) in Boumalne. *Boumalne, Morocco. 1955.*

FIG.107 OPPOSITE BOTTOM Kasbahs in the High Atlas Mountains. *Morocco. 1955.*

FIG.108 ABOVE Gorge in the High Atlas Mountains. *Morocco. 1955.*

FIG.109 OPPOSITE TOP Gorge in the Dades Valley below M'semrir. *Morocco. 1955.*

FIG.110 OPPOSITE BOTTOM Boys on the Ait Abdi plateau. *Morocco. 1955.*

FIG.111 ABOVE Portrait of a shepherd boy. *Morocco. 1955.*

FIG.112 ABOVE Portrait of a girl sitting on a rock. *Ahansal, Morocco. 1955.*

FIG.113 OPPOSITE Kasbah, or fortress, at Ahansal in the High Atlas Mountains. *Ahansal, Morocco. 1955.*

FIG.114 OPPOSITE Portrait of a man carrying a knife. *Morocco. 1955.*

FIG.115 ABOVE Woman, standing in a doorway, wearing beaded
and metal jewellery. *Ahansal, Morocco. 1955.*

FIG.116 ABOVE An elderly Berber man in a village in the High Atlas Mountains. *Morocco. 1955.*

FIG.117 OPPOSITE TOP Houses at a settlement near Assareg on Jebel Toubkal, at 13,671 feet the highest peak in the Atlas Mountains and in North Africa. *Morocco. 1955.*

FIG.118 OPPOSITE BOTTOM Boy with a mule. *Morocco. 1955.*

FIG.119 OPPOSITE TOP The large defensive walls of an unidentified town. *Morocco. 1955.*

FIG.120 OPPOSITE BOTTOM Tuareg men with camels. *Goulimine, Morocco. 1955.*

FIG.121 ABOVE Houses at Assareg in the High Atlas Mountains. *Assareg, Morocco. 1955.*

FIG.122 ABOVE Sheep grazing outside Marrakech, with the snow-covered Atlas Mountains in the distance. *Morocco. 1965.*

FIG.123 OPPOSITE A Berber man on horseback awaiting the arrival of King Hassan II during the Feast of the Throne in Marrakech. *Marrakech, Morocco. 1965.*

FIG.124 OVERLEAF Crowds gathered in Djama el Fna, the main square in Marrakech. *Marrakech, Morocco. 1965.*

FIG.125 OPPOSITE TOP Berber horsemen with rifles during the
Feast of the Throne, the annual celebration marking the accession
of Morocco's ruler. *Marrakech, Morocco. 1965.*

FIG.126 OPPOSITE BOTTOM Berber riders at the annual Feast of the
Throne celebrations. *Morocco. 1968.*

FIG.127 ABOVE Ornate doorway of the fourteenth-century Attarin
Madrasa in Fez. The location of the madrasa (Islamic school) near
the city's spice and perfume market gives al-'Attarin – 'the madrasa
of the perfumers' – its name. *Fez, Morocco. 1965.*

ETHIOPIA

FIG.128 ABOVE The monolithic rock-hewn church of Genete
Mariam, located not far from Lalibela's famous carved churches.
Genete Mariam, Ethiopia. 1959.

FIG.129 OPPOSITE Priest at the entrance of the church known as
Golgotha, one of eleven monolithic rock-hewn churches in Lalibela.
'I was amazed,' Thesiger wrote, 'by the inspiration that had visualized
them, and the craftsmanship that had created them.' *Lalibela,
Ethiopia. 1959.*

FIG.130 OVERLEAF The weekly market in Lalibela. *Lalibela, Ethiopia.
February 1959.*

FIG. 131 OPPOSITE The rock-hewn church of Medhane Alam. Like the other churches in Lalibela, Medhane Alam was made during the thirteenth century, carved in one piece from the rock on which it stands. *Lalibela, Ethiopia. 1959.*

FIG. 132 ABOVE Acolytes at the entrance of the rock-hewn church of Emanuel in Lalibela. *Lalibela, Ethiopia. 1959.*

FIG.133 PREVIOUS PAGES People processing from the church of Gabriel in Lalibela. *Lalibela, Ethiopia. 1960.*

FIG.134 ABOVE People gathered outside the church of Beta Mariam after a Sunday service. *Lalibela, Ethiopia. 1959.*

FIG.135 OPPOSITE A boy, who is probably training for the priesthood, outside the church of Beta Mariam. *Lalibela, Ethiopia. 1959.*

FIG.136 OPPOSITE TOP The market in Batie. *Batie, Ethiopia. 1959.*

FIG.137 OPPOSITE BOTTOM Konso grave marked by carved wooden effigies representing a dead man, flanked by his wives and killed enemies. *Ethiopia. 1959.*

FIG.138 ABOVE Boran woman tying a saddle on to a camel. *Ethiopia. 1959.*

FIG.139 OVERLEAF Houses in the Konso village of Bakawli. The pottery vessels built into the thatched roofs help to seal them from rainwater. *Bakawli, Ethiopia. 1959.*

FIG.140 ABOVE Portrait of a Boran elder. *Ethiopia. 1959.*

FIG.141 OPPOSITE A Fitaurari and his wife whose family entertained
Thesiger during his journey through northern Ethiopia. *Mikri,
Ethiopia. 1960.*

FIG.142 OPPOSITE Portrait of an Amhara man. *Ethiopia. 1960.*

FIG.143 ABOVE A shepherd boy wearing an animal skin over his shoulders. *Ambaras Mikael, Ethiopia. 1960.*

FIG.144 OPPOSITE The great northern escarpment of Ethiopia's Simien Mountains, which Thesiger described as being 'perhaps the most spectacular scene in Africa'. *Ethiopia. 1960.*

FIG.145 ABOVE Giant lobelias growing on Mount Buahit in the Simien Mountains. *Ethiopia. 1960.*

Fig.146 above Group of men in the Ethiopian highlands.
Ethiopia. 1960.

Fig.147 opposite Man holding a large bound volume of religious
texts. Ethiopia has a Christian tradition which dates back to the
fourth century. *Ethiopia. 1960.*

FIG.148 ABOVE People outside the church of Imrahanna Krestos,
built in a cave at Imraha during the twelfth century. *Imraha, Ethiopia.*
1960.

FIG.149 OPPOSITE The entrance of the church of Imrahanna
Krestos. *Imraha, Ethiopia. 1960.*

FIG.150 OVERLEAF View looking north from Tanta, with a boy
standing on rocks in the foreground. *Tanta, Ethiopia. 1960.*

TANZANIA

FIG.151 OPPOSITE A Maasai woman adorned with heavy metal jewellery signifying her status in the community. *Ngorongoro, Tanzania. 1963.*

FIG.152 ABOVE LEFT A young Maasai wearing heavy metal earrings and the black goatskin cape and ostrich feather headdress associated with circumcision. *Ngorongoro Crater, Tanzania. 1961.*

FIG.153 ABOVE RIGHT Portrait of a Maasai *moran* (warrior). *Olbalbal, Tanzania. 1961.*

FIG.154 BELOW LEFT Portrait of a Maasai youth a few hours after his circumcision. *Ngorongoro Crater, Tanzania. 1961.*

FIG.155 BELOW RIGHT A cluster of spears left in the ground while their Maasai owners dance. *Ngorongoro Crater, Tanzania. 1961.*

FIG.156 ABOVE Maasai men dancing at a circumcision ceremony.
Ngorongoro, Tanzania. 1963.

FIG.157 OVERLEAF Maasai dwelling and fenced enclosure in the
northern highlands of Tanzania. *Ololmoti Crater, Tanzania. 1961.*

FIG.158 ABOVE View of Kibo peak on Mount Kilimanjaro
(19,341 feet), the highest mountain in Africa. *Mount Kilimanjaro,
Tanzania. 1962.*

FIG.159 OPPOSITE TOP Maasai men playing the widespread
African game *mancala. Ngorongoro, Tanzania. 1963.*

FIG.160 OPPOSITE BOTTOM A cattle herder on the fertile highlands
around the Ngorongoro Crater. *Ngorongoro, Tanzania. 1963.*

Fig.161 opposite top Maasai women in a *boma* (village),
a settlement comprising several households in the same
enclosure. *Ngorongoro, Tanzania. 1963.*

Fig.162 opposite bottom A Maasai woman and children at
the entrance of a protected settlement. 'Such stockades are built
of juniper posts,' Thesiger noted. *Ngorongoro, Tanzania. 1963.*

Fig.163 above Portrait of a Maasai elder. *Ngorongoro, Tanzania. 1963.*

FIG.164 ABOVE LEFT A young Maasai *moran*, or warrior, wearing a lion's mane headdress. *Simanjiro, Tanzania. 1963.*

FIG.165 ABOVE RIGHT Young Maasai man with matted hair and earrings. *Simanjiro, Tanzania. 1963.*

FIG.166 OPPOSITE TOP On the Maasai Steppe. *Namalulu, Tanzania. 1963.*

FIG.167 OPPOSITE BOTTOM A cattle herder seen through a line of spears. *Ndedo, Tanzania. 1963.*

FIG.168 OPPOSITE An Endo man leaning on his bow, with two
quivers over his shoulder. *Ololmoti, Tanzania. 1963.*

FIG.169 ABOVE Watering cattle at a well. *Kiteto, Tanzania. 1963.*

FIG.170 OVERLEAF Boats in the harbour on the spice island of
Zanzibar. *Zanzibar, Tanzania. 1963.*

KENYA

FIG.171 OPPOSITE Pokot men butchering a zebra shot for them by Thesiger. *Amaya, Kenya. 1961.*

FIG.172 BELOW LEFT A young Turkana man with spears. *Kurungu, Kenya. 1961.*

FIG.173 BELOW RIGHT Portrait of a Turkana elder with metal nose and arm ornaments. *Kerio River, Kenya. 1961.*

FIG.174 ABOVE A Turkana elder. *Kerio River, Kenya. 1961.*

FIG.175 OPPOSITE TOP Boats beached on the island and ancient trading seaport of Lamu. 'It pleased me to be back once more in this Muslim atmosphere,' Thesiger wrote of his visit. The Kenyan mainland is visible in the distance. *Lamu, Kenya. 1961.*

FIG.176 OPPOSITE BOTTOM Samburu families travelling with laden donkeys. *Near Maralal, Kenya. 1962.*

FIG.177 PREVIOUS PAGES Lake Turkana, formerly called Lake Rudolf, seen from its southern end near Teleki's volcano. *Lake Turkana, Kenya. 1962.*

FIG.178 BELOW An ox drinking from a wooden water-trough at Ilaut wells. As pastoralists, the Samburu value their cattle highly, and feeding and watering them remains a large part of the herder's life. *Ilaut, Kenya. 1968–9.*

FIG.179 OPPOSITE TOP Turkana men resting in the shade beneath some trees. *Kerio River, Kenya. 1968–9.*

FIG.180 OPPOSITE BOTTOM Pokot women with the head of a camel which, Thesiger records, had collapsed from illness and was subsequently butchered for food. *Lake Baringo, Kenya. 1968–9.*

FIG. 181 OPPOSITE Goats being led by their Turkana herders to
water at Mouwoligiteng pools near Mount Kulal. *Mouwoligiteng,
Kenya. 1969.*

FIG. 182 ABOVE View of Mount Kenya from the Teleki Valley,
glaciers clearly visible on its slopes, with giant groundsel in the
foreground. *Mount Kenya, Kenya. 1970.*

FIG.183 OPPOSITE Game scouts on Mount Kenya. *Mount Kenya, Kenya. 1970.*

FIG.184 ABOVE A leopard driven off its kill and up a tree by a pride of lions. 'The leopard paid little attention to the lions when it was up the tree,' Thesiger noted, 'but became very savage as soon as I came close to the tree in the Land Rover.' *Maasai Mara National Park, Kenya. 1972.*

FIG.185 PREVIOUS PAGES Trees on the shore of Lake Nakuru, with flamingoes feeding in the distance. *Lake Nakuru, Kenya. 1972.*

FIG.186 BELOW Cattle resting in front of a shelter built for a Samburu circumcision ceremony. 'No boy can be circumcised if his cattle are not in the camp outside his hut,' Thesiger recorded. *Near Maralal, Kenya. 1977.*

FIG.187 ABOVE LEFT Samburu woman shaving her son's head on
the eve of his circumcision. Living intimately with the Samburu for so
many years, Thesiger understood the significance and importance to
them of their circumcision rituals. *Near Maralal, Kenya. 1977.*

FIG.188 ABOVE RIGHT Lawi Leboyare wrapped in the goatskin
cape traditionally worn at the time of circumcision. *Near Maralal,
Kenya. 1977.*

 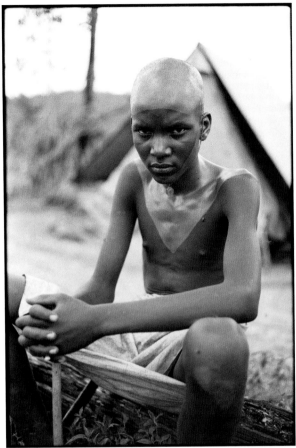

FIG.189 ABOVE LEFT Portrait of a Samburu youth shortly after his circumcision. Around his head are tied the stuffed skins of small birds which he has shot with a bow and blunted arrows. 'After this ceremony, the initiate became a *moran*,' Thesiger noted. *Near Maralal, Kenya. 1977.*

FIG.190 ABOVE RIGHT Portrait of Lawi. *Near Maralal, Kenya. 1977.*

FIG.191 OPPOSITE TOP A young Samburu initiate chanting the *lebarta*, or circumcision song. *Near Maralal, Kenya. 1977.*

FIG.192 OPPOSITE BOTTOM Young Samburu wearing black ostrich feather headdresses and holding bows and blunted arrows for use during the final part of the lengthy circumcision ritual. *Near Maralal, Kenya. 1977.*

FIG.193 ABOVE Young Samburu man. *Near Maralal, Kenya. 1977.*

FIG.194 OPPOSITE A Samburu man, father of a boy called
Kendawa, holding a pottery vessel used to contain beer. *Near
Maralal, Kenya. 1980.*

Fig.195 opposite top Samburu dancing after a circumcision
ceremony. *Near Maralal, Kenya. 1979.*

Fig.196 opposite bottom Two Samburu *moran* braiding another
man's hair. *Near Maralal, Kenya. 1980.*

Fig.197 above left A Samburu *moran*, or warrior, being
decorated with red ochre. *Uaso Nyiro River, Kenya. 1980.*

Fig.198 above right Portrait of a Samburu *moran* (warrior).
He has braided hair, is adorned with red ochre and white markings
on his cheeks, and wears beaded ornaments around his head and
neck. *Near Maralal, Kenya. 1980.*

FIG.199 OPPOSITE TOP Samburu women with their children.
Barsaloi River, Kenya. 1980.

FIG.200 OPPOSITE BOTTOM Samburu dance. *Near Maralal,
Kenya. 1982.*

FIG.201 ABOVE Samburu girls at a dance. *Near Maralal, Kenya. 1983.*

FIG.202 OVERLEAF A Turkana woman, heavily adorned with
beaded neck ornaments, carrying a large gourd on her back.
Loiengalani, Kenya. 1980.

NOTES

Chapter 1

Wilfred Thesiger in Africa

1   Letter from Wilfred Thesiger to Brian Thesiger, 12 November 1930 (Eton College Library).

2   Wilfred Thesiger, *Desert, Marsh and Mountain* (London, 1979), p. 21.

3   Letter from Wilfred Thesiger to Brian Thesiger, 12 November 1930 (Eton College Library).

4   The term Danakil, used widely in the 1930s at the time of Thesiger's journey to refer to the Afar people, was sometimes also used to refer to northern Afar specifically, while southern Afar were sometimes called Adel (or Adal). The Afar were also noted as having two important social classes, the Asaimara ('the red ones') or nobles, and the Adoimara ('the white ones') or commoners. Today the term Afar is preferred to refer to the entire language group.

5   Wilfred Thesiger, *Arabian Sands* (1959), p. 8.

6   Wilfred Thesiger, *The Life of My Choice* (1987), p. 80.

7   Kathleen Mary Thesiger (later Kathleen Mary Astley), unpublished manuscript, undated (private collection).

8   Wilfred Thesiger, conversation with author, 1979.

9   Alexander Maitland, *Wilfred Thesiger: The Life of the Great Explorer* (2006), p. 309.

10 Wilfred Thesiger, *The Life of My Choice* (1987), p. 172.

11 Wilfred Thesiger, *The Danakil Diary* (1996), p. 37.

12 *Ibid.*, pp. 26, 28–9.

13 Wilfred Thesiger, conversation with author; Wilfred Thesiger, *Arabian Sands* (1959), p. 15.

14 Wilfred Thesiger, *The Danakil Diary* (1996), p. 13.

15 Wilfred Thesiger, *Arabian Sands* (1959), p. 7.

16 Wilfred Thesiger, *The Danakil Diary* (1996), p. 37.

17 Alexander Maitland, *Wilfred Thesiger: The Life of the Great Explorer* (2006), p. 91.

18 Letter from C. W. Hobley to Wilfred Thesiger, 30 April 1933 (private collection).

19 Alexander Maitland, *Wilfred Thesiger: The Life of the Great Explorer* (2006), p. 91.

20 *Ibid.*, p. 93.

21 The editors are grateful to Dr Robert Prys-Jones of the Department of Zoology, Natural History Museum (Tring), for his helpful comments on Thesiger's bird collections.

22 Wilfred Thesiger, *The Danakil Diary* (1996), p. 204.

23 Letter from Omar Ibrahim to Wilfred Thesiger, 8 August 1934 (private collection).

24 Wilfred Thesiger, *The Danakil Diary* (1996), p. 204.

25 Wilfred Thesiger, unpublished manuscript 1934 (Eton College Library).

26 Wilfred Thesiger, *The Danakil Diary* (1996), p. 204.

27 *Ibid.*, p. 203.

28 Wilfred Thesiger, conversation with author, 1979; Alexander Maitland, *Wilfred Thesiger: The Life of the Great Explorer* (2006), p. 69.

29 Letter from Wilfred Thesiger to Roderic M. D. Thesiger, 15 July 1936 (Eton College Library).

30 Wilfred Thesiger, *The Life of My Choice* (1987), p. 207.

31 Letter from Wilfred Thesiger to his mother, 16 September 1935 (Eton College Library).

32 W. P. Thesiger, 'Galloping Lion', *Sudan Notes and Records*, vol. 22 (1939), p.157.

33 A. Blayney Percival, *A Game Ranger's Notebook* (1924), p. 56.

34 *Ibid.*

35 Wilfred Thesiger, conversation with author, 1979.

36 Letter from C. W. Hobley to Wilfred Thesiger, 30 April 1933 (private collection).

37 C. G. and B. Z. Seligman, *Pagan Tribes of the Nilotic Sudan* (1932, reissued 1965), p. 145.

38 *Ibid.*, p. 212.

39 Letter from Wilfred Thesiger to his mother, 31 December 1935 (Eton College Library).

40 Alexander Maitland, *Wilfred Thesiger: The Life of the Great Explorer* (2006), p. 174.

41 Wilfred Thesiger, *The Life of My Choice* (1987), p. 209.

42 *Ibid.*, p. 210.

43 Letter from Guy Moore to Wilfred Thesiger, 30 August 1959 (private collection).

44 *Ibid.*

45 Card from Guy Moore to Wilfred Thesiger, inscribed 'GM Christmas 1964' (private collection).

46 Wilfred Thesiger, *The Life of My Choice* (1987), p. 201.

47 *Ibid.*, p. 210.

48 *Ibid.*, p. 214.

49 Letter from Hugh Boustead to Wilfred Thesiger, Tangier, 12 June 1971 (private collection).

50 Wilfred Thesiger, *The Life of My Choice* (1987), p. 251.

51 Mark Leather, unpublished manuscript, 19 August 1937 (private collection).

52 Letter from Wilfred Thesiger to his mother, 19 August 1937 (Eton College Library).

53 Wilfred Thesiger, *The Life of My Choice* (1987), p. 201.

54 *Ibid.*, p. 258.

55 Alexander Maitland, *Wilfred Thesiger: The Life of the Great Explorer* (2006), p. 161.

56 *Ibid.*, p. 97.

57 Wilfred Thesiger, *The Life of My Choice* (1987), p. 246.

58 Letter from Wilfred Thesiger to his mother, 6 November 1938 (Eton College Library).

59 Wilfred Thesiger, unpublished Tibesti report, 26 pp., with manuscript corrections (undated but circa 1938–9) (private collection).

60 Letter from A. J. Arkell to Wilfred Thesiger, Khartoum, 3 February 1939 (private collection).

61 Wilfred Thesiger, Tibesti manuscript and typed carbon copy, undated (private collection).

62 *Ibid.*

63 Sir Mark Allen, in *The Ultimate Traveller* (2003), pp. 9–10.

64 This incident happened in about 1989: Michael Meredith, conversation with author, 2004.

65 Wilfred Thesiger, conversation with author, 1992.

66 Alexander Maitland, *Wilfred Thesiger: The Life of the Great Explorer* (2006), p. 201.

67 Wilfred Thesiger, *The Life of My Choice* (1987), p. 323.

68 Wilfred Thesiger, conversation with author; Letter from Wilfred Thesiger to his mother, 6 February 1945 (Eton College Library); *Alexander Maitland, Wilfred Thesiger: The Life of the Great Explorer* (2006), p. 260.

69 Letter from Wilfred Thesiger to his mother, 18 January 1942 (Eton College Library).

70 Wilfred Thesiger, conversation with author.

71 Letter from Wilfred Thesiger to his mother, 12 December 1944 (Eton College Library).

72 Alexander Maitland, *Wilfred Thesiger: The Life of the Great Explorer* (2006), p. 248.

73 Wilfred Thesiger, *The Life of My Choice* (1987), p. 396.

74 Alexander Maitland, *Wilfred Thesiger: The Life of the Great Explorer* (2006), p. 76.

75 Wilfred Thesiger, *The Life of My Choice* (1987), p. 258.

76 Wilfred Thesiger, Morocco diary, 4 August 1955 (Eton College Library).

77 Ronald Cudrai, quoted by Alexander Maitland in Wilfred Thesiger, *A Vanished World* (2001), p.13.

78 Wilfred Thesiger, Morocco diary, 22 August 1955 (Eton College Library).

79 *Ibid.*, 15 September 1955.

80 Letter from Wilfred Thesiger to Alexander Maitland, 27 April 1965 (private collection).

81 Wilfred Thesiger, conversation with author, 1965.

82 Letter from Claude Auchinleck to Wilfred Thesiger, 14 February 1966 (private collection).

83 Wilfred Thesiger, *The Life of My Choice* (1987), p. 374.

84 Letter from Claude Auchinleck to Wilfred Thesiger, 14 February 1966 (private collection); Wilfred Thesiger, conversation with author.

85 Letter from Wilfred Thesiger to his mother, 6 March 1959 (Eton College Library).

86 Wilfred Thesiger, *The Life of My Choice* (1987), p. 402.

87 *Ibid.*, p. 404.

88 *Ibid.*, p. 424.

89 Wilfred Thesiger, unpublished manuscript (undated but circa 1959) (private collection).

90 *Ibid.*

91 Wilfred G. Thesiger, 'Account of the Newly-discovered Ruins at Sellali', *Man*, vol.13 (1913), pp. 162–4.

92 Wilfred Thesiger, *The Life of My Choice* (1987), p. 77.

93 Letter from W. G. Thesiger to Lady Chelmsford, 14 November 1909 (Eton College Library).

94 Wilfred Thesiger, *The Marsh Arabs* (1964), p. 3.

95 Wilfred Thesiger, *The Life of My Choice* (1987), p. 424.

96 *Ibid.*, p. 429.

97 Wilfred Thesiger, conversation with author, 1992.

98 John Hillaby, *Journey to the Jade Sea* (1964), p. 4.

99 Letter from John Hillaby to Wilfred Thesiger, 6 March 1963 (private collection).

100 Wilfred Thesiger, *My Kenya Days* (1994), p. 17.

101 *Ibid.*, p. 18.

102 *Ibid.*, p. 19.

103 *Ibid.*

104 Alexander Maitland, *Wilfred Thesiger: The Life of the Great Explorer* (2006), p. 392.

105 Letter from John Newbould to Wilfred Thesiger, 18 December 1961 (private collection).

106 Letter from John Newbould to Wilfred Thesiger, 3 December 1961 (private collection).

107 Letter from Wilfred Thesiger to his mother, 25 April 1961 (Eton College Library).

108 Letter from Wilfred Thesiger to his mother, 5 August 1963 (Eton College Library).

109 Wilfred Thesiger, *My Kenya Days* (1994), p. 98.

110 *Ibid.*, p. 205.

111 Wilfred Thesiger, unpublished manuscript (undated but circa 1974) (private collection).

112 *Ibid.*

113 Wilfred Thesiger, unpublished manuscript, 'Masai Method of Circumcision', 1963 (private collection); also compare with photograph in Wilfred Thesiger, *My Kenya Days* (1994), p. 218, and Wilfred Thesiger's notes (undated but circa 1974) (private collection).

114 Letter from Ingaret Giffard to Wilfred Thesiger, 27 July 1963 (private collection).

115 Wilfred Thesiger, *My Kenya Days* (1994), p. 101.

116 Letter from Wilfred Thesiger to his mother, 5 September 1968 (Eton College Library).

117 Letter from Wilfred Thesiger to his mother, 27 September 1968 (Eton College Library).

118 Letter from Wilfred Thesiger to his mother, 12 October 1968 (Eton College Library).

119 Wilfred Thesiger, conversation with author, 1992.

120 Alexander Maitland, *Wilfred Thesiger: A Life in Pictures* (2004), p. 25.

121 Wilfred Thesiger, *My Kenya Days* (1994), p. 206.

122 Alexander Maitland, *Wilfred Thesiger: The Life of the Great Explorer* (2006), p. 172.

123 Wilfred Thesiger, *My Kenya Days* (1994), p. 52.

124 *Ibid.*, pp. 150–1.

125 Wilfred Thesiger, conversation with author, 1992.

126 Letter from Wilfred Thesiger to his mother, 11 January 1961 (Eton College Library).

127 Wilfred Thesiger, conversation with author, 1979.

128 Wilfred Thesiger, *The Danakil Diary* (1996), p. 138.

129 Letter from Wilfred Thesiger to his mother, 16 December 1960 (Eton College Library).

130 Wilfred Thesiger, *My Kenya Days* (1994), p. 147.

131 Eric Shipton, *Upon That Mountain* (1943), p. 52.

132 Wilfred Thesiger, conversation with author, 1993.

133 Wilfred Thesiger, *My Kenya Days* (1994), p. 210.

134 Wilfred Thesiger, conversation with author, 1979.

135 Wilfred Thesiger, conversation with author; and also see Wilfred Thesiger, *A Vanished World* (2001), p. 10.

136 H. M. Hyatt, *The Church of Abyssinia* (1928), pp. 169–70.

137 Wilfred Thesiger, *The Danakil Diary* (1996), p. 56.

138 *Ibid.*, p. 102.

139 *Ibid.*

140 Wilfred Thesiger, *My Kenya Days* (1994), p. 33.

141 Wilfred Thesiger, *Visions of a Nomad* (1987), p. 10.

142 Letter from Wilfred Thesiger to his mother, 31 January 1934 (Eton College Library).

143 Against the total payment of £118 5s. 6d. Sinclair's allowed Thesiger £65 for the Leica IIIb and its 50 mm lens in part-exchange for the Leica M3 (James Sinclair & Co. Ltd. invoices: private collection).

144 Wilfred Thesiger, conversation with author, 1992.

145 Wilfred Thesiger, conversation with author.

Chapter 3

Wilfred Thesiger: Last of the Gentleman Travellers

1 Eric Newby, *A Short Walk in the Hindu Kush* (1958), p. 246.

2 *Ibid.*, p. 248.

3 Evelyn Waugh, Preface to Eric Newby, *A Short Walk in the Hindu Kush* (1958), p. 11.

4 Eric Newby, *A Short Walk in the Hindu Kush* (1958), p. 246.

5 Wilfred Thesiger, *The Life of My Choice* (1987), p. 212.

6 Wilfred Thesiger, *Arabian Sands* (1959), p. 82.

Chapter 4

Imagined Time: Thesiger, Photography and the Past

1 Deborah Poole, 'An Excess of Description: Ethnography, Race, and Visual Technologies', *Annual Review of Anthropology*, vol. 34 (2005), p. 172.

2 Edward Weston quoted in E. Jussim and E. Lindquist-Cock, *Landscape as Photograph* (1985), pp. 86–7.

3 Wilfred Thesiger, *Visions of a Nomad* (1987), p. 11.

4 Wilfred Thesiger, personal communication.

5 R. Rosaldo, 'From the Door of his Tent', in J. Clifford and G. E. Marcus (eds.), *Writing Culture: The Poetics and Politics of Ethnography* (1986), pp. 96–7.

6 J. Clifford, 'On Ethnographic Allegory', in J. Clifford and G. E. Marcus (eds.), *Writing Culture: The Poetics and Politics of Ethnography* (1986), pp. 114–15.

7 Wilfred Thesiger, *Visions of a Nomad* (1987), p. 10.

8 David E. Nye, 'Visualising Eternity: Photographic Constructions of the Grand Canyon', in J. Schwartz and J. Ryan (eds.), *Picturing Place: Photography and the Geographical Imagination* (2003), pp. 90–4.

9 Wilfred Thesiger, *Visions of a Nomad* (1987), p. 12.

Chapter 5

An Incidental Collection: Objects Donated by Wilfred Thesiger to the Pitt Rivers Museum

1 Given Thesiger's repeatedly expressed childhood enjoyment of Major Percy Horace Gordon Powell-Cotton's *A Sporting Trip through Abyssinia* (1902), he would no doubt have appreciated the fact that the next collection Penniman registered was one, transferred from the Powell-Cotton Museum at Quex Park in Birchington-on-Sea, Kent, that had been acquired by Powell-Cotton's daughters Antoinette and Diana in Angola in 1936–7.

2 The records for all the items in 'the Thesiger collection' may be found in the relevant entries in the regularly updated version of the Museum's database available online at http://www.prm.ox.ac.uk/databases.html.

3 Wilfred Thesiger, Foreword to *Wilfred Thesiger's Photographs: A 'Most Cherished Possession'* (1993), (unpaginated).

4 Wilfred Thesiger, *The Danakil Diary* (1996), p. 88.

5 T. K. Penniman, *Report of the Curator of the Pitt*

Rivers Museum (Department of Ethnology) for the Two Years Ending 31 July 1946 (1946), p. 7.

6   Wilfred Thesiger, *The Life of My Choice* (1987), p. 80.

7   *Ibid.*, p. 27.

8   *Ibid.*, p. 26.

9   *Ibid.*, p. 52.

10 Wilfred Thesiger, *The Danakil Diary* (1996), p. 128.

11 *Ibid.*, p. 198.

12 *Ibid.*, p. 186.

13 For logistical reasons, these latter two collections were formally accessioned together in 1995 as collection 1995.5.

14 Alexander Maitland, *Wilfred Thesiger: The Life of the Great Explorer* (2006), p. 14.

15 From notes supplied to the Museum by Alexander Maitland in 2009, held in the related documents file for Museum collection 1998.28.

16 Wilfred Thesiger, *Visions of a Nomad* (1987), p. 10.

17 Alexander Maitland, *Wilfred Thesiger: The Life of the Great Explorer* (2006), p. 415.

18 Wilfred Thesiger, *The Life of My Choice* (1987), p. 59.

19 Alexander Maitland, *Wilfred Thesiger: The Life of the Great Explorer* (2006), p. 2.

20 See, for example, W. Thesiger and M. Meynell, 'On a Collection of Birds from Danakil, Abyssinia', *Ibis*, vol. 77 (1935), pp. 774–807.

21 Wilfred Thesiger, *Visions of a Nomad* (1987), p. 10.

22 Ian Fairservice, 'Introduction', in *The Thesiger Collection: A Catalogue of Unique Photographs by Wilfred Thesiger* (1991), p. 3.

Chapter 6

Wilfred Thesiger's Photograph Collection at the Pitt Rivers Museum

1   Document dated January 1992 (Pitt Rivers Museum).

2   Letter from Frank Steele to Pitt Rivers Museum, 28 March 1992 (Pitt Rivers Museum).

3   From a document enclosed with a letter from Elizabeth Edwards to Frank Steele, dated 24 February 1993 (Pitt Rivers Museum).

4   Letter from Frank Steele to Elizabeth Edwards, 25 March 1993 (Pitt Rivers Museum).

5   Wilfred Thesiger, *My Kenya Days* (1994), p. 148. Although Thesiger notes that this incident with the Maasai happened during his journey with John Newbould to Tanzania in 1963, it was almost certainly during the slightly earlier journey around Ngorongoro Crater with Newbould in 1961.

6   Wilfred Thesiger, Foreword to *Wilfred Thesiger's Photographs: A 'Most Cherished Possession'* (1993), (unpaginated).

7   Wilfred Thesiger, *My Kenya Days* (1994), p. xi.

8   Letter from Sean Williams (British Council) to Elizabeth Edwards, 4 January 1996 (Pitt Rivers Museum).

9   Elizabeth Edwards, personal communication, 24 July 2009.

10 File note, 30 August 1995 (Pitt Rivers Museum).

11 Letter from Elizabeth Edwards to Sean Williams (British Council), 20 November 1995 (Pitt Rivers Museum).

12 *Ibid.*

13 The Fox Talbot Museum celebrates the life and work of William Henry Fox Talbot (1800–77), owner and resident of Lacock Abbey, Wiltshire, whose experiments in the mid-1830s led him to discover the negative/positive photographic process.

14 This date accounts for the Museum's accession numbers for the collection: 2004.130 (negatives and prints); 2004.131 (albums).

15 The exhibition was jointly curated by Elin Bornemann, Jocelyne Dudding, Elizabeth Edwards, Philip Grover and Alex Nadin, all of the Pitt Rivers Museum.

16 Letter from Graham Heard (National Trust) to Elizabeth Edwards, 5 August 2004 (Pitt Rivers Museum).

17 Document, 27 February 2007 (Pitt Rivers Museum).

18 Wilfred Thesiger, Foreword to Nigel Pavitt, *Samburu* (1991), p. 6.

19 *Ibid.*, p. 7.

Chapter 7

Wilfred Thesiger's Photographs of Africa: A Centenary Selection

1   Wilfred Thesiger, *My Kenya Days* (1994), p. 1.
2   We have decided to group the first section of Thesiger's photographs of Ethiopia under the title Abyssinia, since this was the name of the country until 1944, and to distinguish them from those in the later section taken after his return to Ethiopia in 1959.
3   Although separately known as Tanganyika and Zanzibar during the period in which Thesiger took his photographs, we have decided to group them under the country's present name of Tanzania to avoid confusion.
4   Wilfred Thesiger, 'An Abyssinian Quest: A Sultan in the Jungle: III – Fauna near Aussa', *The Times*, 2 August 1934, pp. 11–12, 14; Wilfred Thesiger, 'The Awash River and the Aussa Sultanate', *Geographical Journal*, vol. 85 (1935), pp. 1–19; W. Thesiger and M. Meynell, 'On a Collection of Birds from Danakil, Abyssinia', *Ibis*, vol. 77 (1935), pp. 774–807.
5   It is worth noting that all of Thesiger's books and articles – with the exception of only two lecture transcripts, published in *The Journal of the Royal Central Asian Society*, and a short note in the *East African Wildlife Journal* – included his photographs.
6   Wilfred Thesiger, *Desert, Marsh and Mountain* (1979); Wilfred Thesiger, *Visions of a Nomad* (1987).
7   Wilfred Thesiger, *A Vanished World* (2001).
8   Wilfred Thesiger, *Crossing the Sands* (1999).

Bibliography of Works by Sir Wilfred Thesiger (1910–2003)

COMPILED BY PHILIP N. GROVER

Wilfred Thesiger, 'An Abyssinian Quest: I – Finding a Lost River: In Unknown Aussa', *The Times*, 31 July 1934, pp. 15–16.

Wilfred Thesiger, 'An Abyssinian Quest: II – Customs of the Danakil: Tribal Ceremonies', *The Times*, 1 August 1934, pp. 13–14.

Wilfred Thesiger, 'An Abyssinian Quest: A Sultan in the Jungle: III – Fauna near Aussa', *The Times*, 2 August 1934, pp. 11–12.

Wilfred Thesiger, 'An Abyssinian Quest: The Lost Reaches of the Rivers: IV – Salt as Currency', *The Times*, 3 August 1934, pp. 13–14.

Wilfred Thesiger, 'The Awash River and the Aussa Sultanate', *Geographical Journal*, vol. 85 (1935), pp. 1–19.

W. Thesiger and M. Meynell, 'On a Collection of Birds from Danakil, Abyssinia', *Ibis*, vol. 77 (1935), pp. 774–807.

[Wilfred Thesiger], 'The Mind of the Moor: France in North Africa: Nationalist Needs', *The Times*, 21 December 1937, pp. 15–16.

Wilfred Thesiger, 'A Camel Journey to Tibesti', *Geographical Journal*, vol. 94 (1939), pp. 433–46.

W. P. Thesiger, 'Galloping Lion', *Sudan Notes and Records*, vol. 22 (1939), pp. 155–7.

Wilfred Thesiger, 'A New Journey in Southern Arabia', *Geographical Journal*, vol. 108 (1946), pp. 129–45.

W. Thesiger, 'A Journey through the Tihama, the 'Asir, and the Hijaz Mountains', *Geographical Journal*, vol. 110 (1947), pp. 188–200.

Wilfred Thesiger, 'Empty Quarter of Arabia', *Listener*, vol. 38 (1947), pp. 971–2.

W. Thesiger, 'Across the Empty Quarter', *Geographical Journal*, vol. 111 (1948), pp. 1–19.

Wilfred Thesiger, 'Studies in the Southern Hejaz and Tihama', *Geographical Magazine*, vol. 21 (1948–9), p. 8.

Wilfred Thesiger, 'Sands of the Empty Quarter', *Geographical Magazine*, vol. 21 (1948–9), p. 312.

W. Thesiger, 'A Further Journey across the Empty Quarter', *Geographical Journal*, vol. 113 (1949), pp. 21–44.

Wilfred Thesiger, 'Wolves of the Desert: The Sa'ar Tribe at the Watering Place', *Geographical Magazine*, vol. 21 (1948–9), pp. 394–400.

Wilfred Thesiger, 'Travel on the Trucial Coast', *Geographical Magazine*, vol. 22 (1949–50), pp. 110–18.

Wilfred Thesiger, 'The Quicksands of Oman', *Listener*, vol. 42 (1949), pp. 436–8.

Wilfred Thesiger, 'Hawking in Arabia', *Listener*, vol. 42 (1949), pp. 803–4.

W. P. Thesiger, 'The Badu of Southern Arabia', *Journal of the Royal Central Asian Society*, vol. 37 (1950), pp. 53–61.

Wilfred Thesiger, 'Desert Borderlands of Oman', *Geographical Journal*, vol. 116 (1950), pp. 137–68.

Wilfred Thesiger, 'Obituary: Bertram Sidney Thomas, C.M.G., O.B.E.', *Geographical Journal*, vol. 117 (1951), pp. 117–19.

Wilfred Thesiger, 'The Ma'dan or Marsh Dwellers of Southern Iraq', *Journal of the Royal Central Asian Society*, vol. 41 (1954), pp. 4–25.

Wilfred Thesiger, 'The Marsh Arabs of Iraq', *Geographical Magazine*, vol. 27 (1954–5), pp. 138–44.

Wilfred Thesiger, 'The Marshmen of Southern Iraq', *Geographical Journal*, vol. 120 (1954), pp. 272–81.

Wilfred Thesiger, 'In the Kurdish Mountains', *Geographical Magazine*, vol. 27 (1954–5), pp. 599–606.

Wilfred Thesiger, 'The Hazaras of Central Afghanistan', *Geographical Journal*, vol. 121 (1955), pp. 312–19.

Wilfred Thesiger, 'A Journey in Nuristan', *Geographical Journal*, vol. 123 (1957), pp. 457–64.

Wilfred Thesiger, 'Marsh Dwellers of Southern Iraq', *National Geographic Magazine*, vol. 113 (1958), pp. 204–39.

Wilfred Thesiger, *Arabian Sands* (London, 1959).

Wilfred Thesiger, 'Obituary: H. St. John B. Philby, 1885–1960', *Geographical Journal*, vol. 126 (1960), pp. 563–5.

Wilfred Thesiger, *The Marsh Arabs* (London, 1964).

Wilfred Thesiger, Foreword to Neil ffrench Blake, *Handbook for Adventure* (London, 1965), pp. 9–10.

Wilfred Thesiger, 'War in Yemen – 1: Disenchantment with the Egyptians', *The Times*, 21 December 1966, p. 9.

Wilfred Thesiger, 'War in Yemen – 2: Tribesmen Acknowledge the Imam's Rule', *The Times*, 22 December 1966, p. 11.

Wilfred Thesiger, 'Wild Dog at 5894 m (19,340 ft)', *East African Wildlife Journal*, vol. 8 (1970), pp. 202–3.

Wilfred Thesiger, *Desert, Marsh and Mountain: The World of a Nomad* (London, 1979).

Wilfred Thesiger, Foreword to Mark Allen, *Falconry in Arabia* (London, 1980), p. 9.

Wilfred Thesiger, *The Life of My Choice* (London, 1987).

Wilfred Thesiger, *Visions of a Nomad* (London, 1987).

Wilfred Thesiger, Foreword to Hilary Hook, *Home from the Hill* (London, 1987), pp. ix–x.

Wilfred Thesiger, Foreword to Nigel Pavitt, *Kenya: The First Explorers* (London, 1989), pp. 7–10.

Wilfred Thesiger, Foreword to Stephen Taylor, *The Mighty Nimrod: A Life of Frederick Courteney Selous, African Hunter and Adventurer, 1851–1917* (London, 1989), p. xi.

Wilfred Thesiger, Foreword to Clinton Bailey, *Bedouin Poetry from Sinai and the Negev: Mirror of a Culture* (Oxford, 1991), pp. vii–x.

Wilfred Thesiger, Foreword to Nigel Pavitt, *Samburu* (London, 1991), pp. 6–7.

Wilfred Thesiger, Foreword to John Keay (ed.), *The Robinson Book of Exploration* (London, 1993), pp. ix–x.

Wilfred Thesiger, *My Kenya Days* (London, 1994).

Wilfred Thesiger, *The Danakil Diary: Journeys through Abyssinia, 1930–34* (London, 1996).

Wilfred Thesiger, *Among the Mountains: Travels through Asia* (London, 1998).

Wilfred Thesiger, *Crossing the Sands* (Dubai, 1999).

Wilfred Thesiger, Foreword to Bruce Kirkby, *Sand Dance: By Camel across Arabia's Great Southern Desert* (Toronto, 2000), p. ix.

Wilfred Thesiger, Foreword to T. E. Lawrence, *Seven Pillars of Wisdom: A Triumph* (London, 2000), p. xv.

Wilfred Thesiger, *A Vanished World* (London, 2001).

Wilfred Thesiger, *My Life and Travels: An Anthology*, ed. Alexander Maitland (London, 2002).

Photographic Acknowledgements

All photographs in this book are by Wilfred Thesiger, and copyright Pitt Rivers Museum, University of Oxford, unless otherwise stated. The Thesiger Collection was accepted in lieu of inheritance tax by H. M. Government, and allocated to the Pitt Rivers Museum in 2004. All of the photographs for this book have been newly scanned and restored from Wilfred Thesiger's original negatives and albums, and the editors are extremely grateful to Adrian Arbib and Malcolm Osman for their work on the original material. The editors would also like to thank the following copyright holders for permission to reproduce several additional images: Abu Dhabi Authority for Culture and Heritage (Fig. 67), Adrian Arbib (Fig. 51), Alistair Morrison (Fig. 37) and the Royal Geographical Society (Fig. 8).

The Pitt Rivers Museum's accession numbers for the photographs and objects reproduced in this book are:
Fig. 1, 2004.131.70.31; Fig. 2, 2004.131.70.66; Fig. 3, 2004.131.67.59;
Fig. 4, 2004.131.67.37; Fig. 5, 2004.131.67.129; Fig. 6, 2004.131.68.13;
Fig. 7, 2004.130.39250.1; Fig. 9, 2004.130.39256.1; Fig. 10, 2004.130.39251.1;
Fig. 11, 2004.130.39259.1, 2004.130.39260.1; Fig. 12, 2004.130.32783.1;
Fig. 13, 2004.131.71.89; Fig. 14, 2004.130.34523.1; Fig. 15, 2004.130.36228.1;
Fig. 16, 2004.130.36262.1; Fig. 17, 2004.130.36667.1; Fig. 18, 2004.131.3.3;
Fig. 19, 2004.130.35865.1; Fig. 20, 2004.130.10761.1; Fig. 21, 2004.130.2373.1;
Fig. 22, 2004.131.45.19; Fig. 23, 2004.130.37189.1; Fig. 24, 2004.130.37687.1;
Fig. 25, 2004.130.23529.1; Fig. 26, 2004.130.23660.1; Fig. 27, 2004.130.23803.1;
Fig. 28, 2004.130.27536.1; Fig. 29, 2004.130.27771.1; Fig. 30, 2004.130.30873.1;
Fig. 31, 2004.130.1662.1; Fig. 32, 2004.130.30802.1; Fig. 33, 2004.130.1453.1;
Fig. 34, 2004.130.2146.1; Fig. 35, 2004.130.21505.1; Fig. 36, 2004.130.26052.1;
Fig. 38, 2004.130.36563.1; Fig. 39, 2004.130.32682.1; Fig. 40, 2004.130.32875.1;
Fig. 41, 2004.130.32940.1; Fig. 42, 2004.130.26195.1; Fig. 43, 2004.131.67.32;
Fig. 44, 2004.131.70.1 (inside front cover); Fig. 45, 2004.131.70.2;
Fig. 46, 2004.130.39253; Fig. 47, 2004.130.39252.1; Fig. 48, 2004.130.17101.1;
Fig. 49, 2004.130.32495.1; Fig. 50, 2004.130.36995.1; Fig. 52, 2004.130.8708.1;
Fig. 53, 2004.130.30177.1; Fig. 54, 2004.130.23753.1; Fig. 55, 1945.9.32

(photograph by Malcolm Osman); Fig. 56, 1945.9.75 (photograph by Malcolm Osman); Fig. 57, 1945.9.82 (photograph by Malcolm Osman); Fig. 58, 2004.131.71.9; Fig. 59, 1945.9.78 (top), 1945.9.79 (bottom) (photograph by Malcolm Osman); Fig. 60, 1995.5.3 (photograph by Malcolm Osman); Fig. 61, 1998.26.21 (left), 1998.26.22 (centre), 1998.26.23 (right) (photograph by Malcolm Osman); Fig. 62, 1998.435.2.3.2; Fig. 63, 2004.131.70.37 – .46; Fig. 64, 1998.303.12.13; Fig. 65, Museum reference A23.F31.3; Fig. 66, 1998.435.14.4; Fig. 68, 2004.131.67.56; Fig. 69, 2004.131.67.57; Fig. 70, 2004.131.68.43; Fig. 71, 2004.130.31099.1; Fig. 72, 2004.131.70.45; Fig. 73, 2004.130.39248; Fig. 74, 2004.130.39249.1; Fig. 75, 2004.130.39255; Fig. 76, 2004.130.39257.1; Fig. 77, 2004.130.35771.1; Fig. 78, 2004.130.38174.1; Fig. 79, 2004.130.38161.1; Fig. 80, 2004.130.36282.1; Fig. 81, 2004.130.36363.1; Fig. 82, 2004.130.36373.1; Fig. 83, 2004.130.36243.1; Fig. 84, 2004.130.32802.1; Fig. 85, 2004.130.36549.1; Fig. 86, 2004.130.32859.1; Fig. 87, 2004.130.32850.1; Fig. 88, 2004.130.36515.1; Fig. 89, 2004.130.36531.1; Fig. 90, 2004.130.36614.1; Fig. 91, 2004.130.36718.1; Fig. 92, 2004.130.36643.1; Fig. 93, 2004.130.36633.1; Fig. 94, 2004.130.36630.1; Fig. 95, 2004.130.36623.1; Fig. 96, 2004.131.71.169; Fig. 97, 2004.131.71.179; Fig. 98, 2004.130.10800.1; Fig. 99, 2004.130.10749.1; Fig. 100, 2004.130.10813.1; Fig. 101, 2004.130.10839.1; Fig. 102, 2004.130.10769.1; Fig. 103, 2004.130.10851.1; Fig. 104, 2004.130.10861.1; Fig. 105, 2004.130.10872.1; Fig. 106, 2004.130.10879.1; Fig. 107, 2004.130.10896.1; Fig. 108, 2004.130.10899.1; Fig. 109, 2004.130.10888.1; Fig. 110, 2004.130.10943.1; Fig. 111, 2004.130.10928.1; Fig. 112, 2004.130.11000.1; Fig. 113, 2004.130.10980.1; Fig. 114, 2004.130.13081.1; Fig. 115, 2004.130.13069.1; Fig. 116, 2004.130.13121.1; Fig. 117, 2004.130.13122.1; Fig. 118, 2004.130.13125.1; Fig. 119, 2004.130.13245.1; Fig. 120, 2004.130.13296.1; Fig. 121, 2004.130.13134.1; Fig. 122, 2004.130.2442.1; Fig. 123, 2004.130.4035.1; Fig. 124, 2004.130.2465.1; Fig. 125, 2004.130.4062.1; Fig. 126, 2004.130.20263.1; Fig. 127, 2004.130.4274.1; Fig. 128, 2004.130.37074.1; Fig. 129, 2004.130.37181.1; Fig. 130, 2004.130.37156.1; Fig. 131, 2004.130.37203.1; Fig. 132, 2004.130.37196.1; Fig. 133, 2004.130.23441.1; Fig. 134, 2004.130.37261.1; Fig. 135, 2004.130.37175.1; Fig. 136, 2004.130.37289.1; Fig. 137, 2004.130.37683.1; Fig. 138, 2004.130.37711.1; Fig. 139, 2004.130.37588.1; Fig. 140, 2004.130.37706.1; Fig. 141, 2004.130.23619.1; Fig. 142, 2004.130.23878.1; Fig. 143, 2004.130.23962.1; Fig. 144, 2004.130.23923.1; Fig. 145, 2004.130.23996.1; Fig. 146, 2004.130.27199.1; Fig. 147, 2004.130.27252.1; Fig. 148, 2004.130.27354.1; Fig. 149, 2004.130.27350.1; Fig. 150, 2004.130.27508.1; Fig. 151, 2004.130.1298.1; Fig. 152, 2004.130.30717.1; Fig. 153, 2004.130.30605.1; Fig. 154, 2004.130.30726.1; Fig. 155, 30721.1; Fig. 156, 2004.130.1285.1; Fig. 157, 2004.130.30789.1; Fig. 158, 2004.130.33442.1; Fig. 159, 2004.130.1024.1; Fig. 160, 2004.130.1202.1; Fig. 161, 2004.130.1317.1; Fig. 162, 2004.130.1020.1; Fig. 163, 2004.130.1354.1; Fig. 164, 2004.130.1458.1; Fig. 165, 2004.130.1474.1; Fig. 166, 2004.130.1521.1; Fig. 167, 2004.130.1766.1; Fig. 168, 2004.130.1911.1; Fig. 169, 2004.130.1973.1; Fig. 170, 2004.130.2125.1; Fig. 171, 2004.130.30524.1; Fig. 172, 2004.130.27997.1; Fig. 173, 2004.130.30279.1; Fig. 174, 2004.130.30285.1; Fig. 175, 2004.130.33434.1; Fig. 176, 2004.130.35136.1; Fig. 177, 2004.130.33684.1; Fig. 178, 2004.130.20440.1; Fig. 179, 2004.130.20492.1; Fig. 180, 2004.130.20752.1; Fig. 181, 2004.130.21027.1; Fig. 182, 2004.130.21941.1; Fig. 183, 2004.130.21852.1; Fig. 184, 2004.130.9982.1; Fig. 185, 2004.130.11110.1; Fig. 186, 2004.130.15052.1; Fig. 187, 2004.130.15301.1; Fig. 188, 2004.130.15086.1; Fig. 189, 2004.130.15468.1; Fig. 190, 2004.130.15367.1; Fig. 191, 2004.130.15166.1; Fig. 192, 2004.130.15232.1; Fig. 193, 2004.130.15399.1; Fig. 194, 2004.130.24617.1; Fig. 195, 2004.130.24116.1; Fig. 196, 2004.130.24608.1; Fig. 197, 2004.130.24481.1; Fig. 198, 2004.130.24644.1; Fig. 199, 2004.130.24841.1; Fig. 200, 2004.130.26187.1; Fig. 201, 2004.130.26361.1; Fig. 202, 2004.130.24692.1.

Index

Entries in *italics* indicate photographs, WT indicates Wilfred Thesiger.